HISTORY OF BOXING

HISTORY OF BOXING

MICHAEL HEATLEY & IAN WELCH

SELECT EDITIONS

All photographs from the Bison Picture Library.

This edition first published in 1997 by the
Promotional Reprint Company Ltd,
Kiln House, 210 New Kings Road, London SW6 4NZ
exclusively for Selecta Book Ltd, Folly Road, Roundway, Devizes, Wiltshire SN10 2HR

ISBN **1 85648 425 4**

Printed and bound in China

Contents

History of Boxing

SOME sports have evolved over time from something quite different, while others — like rugby — owe their genesis to a change of rules in an existing game. Still more, though fewer in number, were invented from scratch, like basketball. Yet few sports can boast as long a history as boxing. Unarmed combat is as old as mankind itself, making boxing and wrestling two of the longest-lived sports that still exist today.

Yet the intervention of the eighth Marquess of Queensberry was crucial in the shaping of the modern sport. The concept of the Queensberry Rules dates back to 1867, when it replaced with boxing of the gloved variety the then-widespread bare-knuckle fighting, similarly drawing up specific conditions of victory and defeat.

Until this point, fights had been fought to the finish no matter how long it took. Now, scoring would be by three-minute rounds, each separated by a minute's break, and the referee was the sole scoring authority. More complex points' systems involving judges have since supplanted this simple system, at least on the world stage, but the common-sense basis certainly civilised the sport. Last, but not least, the contestants had to wear 'fair-sized boxing gloves of the best quality.'

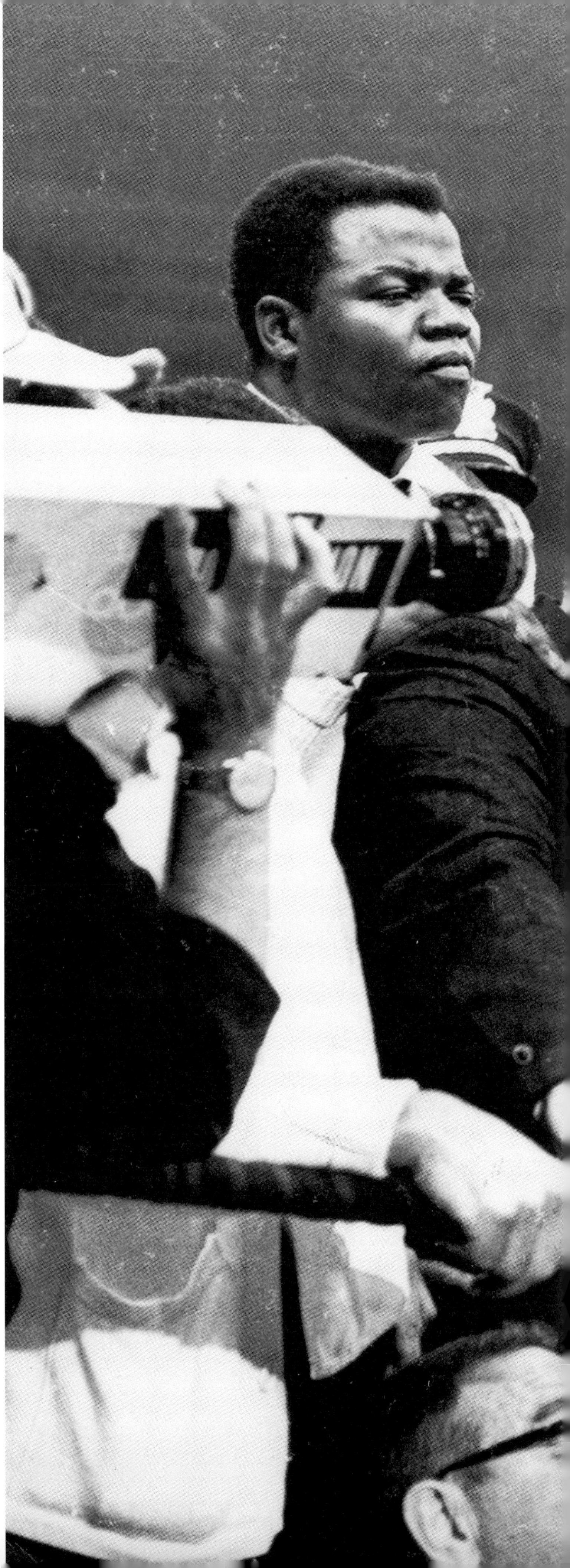

The Greatest — Muhammad Ali, or rather Cassius Clay as he was when this picture was taken in 1965, after the second fight against 'Sonny' Liston confirmed that he wasn't a flash in the pan.

EVERLAST

The very first world championship to be fought under the Queensberry Rules took place in 1884, when 'Nonpariel' Jack Dempsey beat George Fulljames in New York, the Irishman carrying off the middleweight title as a result of a bout that lasted all of nine minutes. It was the first of a catalogue of titles that has, unsatisfactorily to most, mushroomed in recent years as a succession of rival bodies attempting to govern the sport has raised the arm of their respective champions.

The oldest bodies to govern the sport of boxing came into being in the years following World War 1. First to arrive on the scene, in 1920, was the National Boxing Association, which changed its appellation 42 years later to World Boxing Association (WBA), by which we know it today. In Britain, the British Boxing Board of Control, founded in 1929, remains paramount in the fight game, having assumed that mantle from the National Sporting Club.

Then came confusion: the World Boxing Council (WBC) came into being in 1963 in Mexico City, to be joined two decades later by the International Boxing Federation (IBF). Finally, for the present anyway, the World Boxing Organisation (WBO) stepped into the ring in 1988. So today we have the WBA, WBC, IBF and WBO, all of which recognise their own title-holders.

The weight divisions in which the appointed fighters contest these titles are rather less controversial. The main weights have remained unaltered since 1910, and are as follows:

Heavyweight	215lb
Light-heavyweight	175lb
Middleweight	154lb
Welterweight	142lb
Lightweight	133lb
Bantamweight	122lb
Flyweight	116lb

Inevitably, it was the heavyweight division that would inspire the most interest and the biggest headlines in the years that followed. Fighters would trade up weights through the years as they found it more difficult to beat the limits, while in-between categories would arise such as cruiserweight (also known as junior-heavyweight), super (junior) middleweight, etc.

It's impossible these days to imagine a newspaper without at least some mention of boxing in its back pages. The first printed evidence of the sport to survive today dates from January 1681, when a prize fight was reported in the Protestant Mercury. That the sport was at this point on an upswing is undoubted, for by the 1720s boxing was so popular among the common man that King George I had a ring constructed for the public to use in London's Hyde Park.

The first British champion, James Figg, was crowned in 1719, having issued a calling card engraved by William Hogarth claiming he 'teached fencing, singlestick and boxing'. He cashed in on his fame by opening his own academy in central London dedicated to teaching 'the manly arts of foul play, backsword, cudgelling and boxing.' Yet, as the order of that list

hints, fighting with the fists was still very much subservient to the use of cudgels (clubs) and backswords, a practice weapon with just one cutting edge.

Jack Randall (left) and Turner sparring at the Fives Court, a popular boxing venue in the early 19th century. 90 years before Jack Dempsey was given the nickname, Randall was the original 'Nonpareil'.

Figg gave way in 1734 to one George Taylor, but it was his successor Jack Broughton, known as the 'Father of Boxing', who made the more lasting mark. Broughton has been credited with reversing the right foot forward stance boxing had inherited from fencing to lead with the left — the standard right-hander's tactic to this day. He also pioneered the use of gloves (then known as mufflers).

It was Broughton, too, who, over a century before the Queensberry Rules, introduced the first written set of rules, seven in number, to regulate prizefighting. These stated among other things that there should be two umpires to see fair play, that half a minute's break should be observed between rounds and that no-one should be hit when they were down. His innovation was actually born of tragedy: a fighter named George Stevenson having accidentally died at Broughton's own hands.

This first loss of life doubtless brought a wave of public protest, as would each succeeding tragedy to the present day. Though ever more stringent medical safeguards, combined with advances in glove technology, should have rendered boxing ever safer, the fact remains that a physical contact sport will always contain an element of risk.

Though it's clear from Egyptian hieroglyphs that bare-knuckle fighting had existed since 5,000BC, the use of leather or hide to cover the hands was documented by Homer in *The Iliad*. A deadly alternative used in the early Olympics by gladiators was the metal-studded cestus, though the barbarous spectacle that resulted barely qualifies as boxing. Bare-knuckle, though, would remain the norm for many centuries.

Three years after Jack Broughton placed a newspaper advertisement in 1847 asking anyone 'willing to be instructed in the mystery of boxing' to join his academy, he was defeated by Jack Slack. Rather than attempt to regain his crown, he became a full-time promoter, opening a boxing arena confusingly named the 'Tennis Court' in London's Haymarket.

At this point, the sport enjoyed its greatest popularity as an event on which money could be wagered. Elsewhere, boxing was a sideshow, and boxing booths where any would-be challenger could pit his wits against the resident champion were commonplace in travelling fairs worldwide.

Broughton had been backed against Slack by the Duke of Cumberland, a wealthy patron. His Lordship's five-figure loss turned him against boxing with a

An engraving by J. R. Mackrell and J. B. Rowbotham of a fight between Sayers (right) and Heenan. The 17 April 1860 fight attracted huge crowds who saw a drawn match after some 2hr 20min of boxing.

Tom Cribb (right) challenged by Tom Molineaux, a former slave, in 1810. Molineaux put up a tremendous fight but lost in 39 rounds.

vengeance, and he managed to get Parliament to ban the sport — a trend that continues to this day though usually on health grounds.

The following century saw a procession of names stand atop the British boxing ladder. Daniel Mendoza, known as the 'Light of Israel' because of his Jewish descent, and Richard 'The Gentleman' Humphries contested a trio of hard-fought bouts between 1788 and 1790 which put the former well and truly on the map. His quickness of both feet and thought did for many a larger opponent and neatly underlined the fact that there was an alternative to brute strength.

John Jackson, the man who ended Mendoza's reign in 1795 in just 10½ minutes, would become one of the great names of 19th century boxing. As the son of a well-to-do builder, he rejoiced in the nickname 'Gentleman', and earned it: he was noticeably reluctant to deliver the knockout blow to Mendoza on their meeting, having brought his opponent to the edge of defeat in just over 10 minutes.

Finish the job he did, though, and ruled British boxing until the turn of the century. So dominant was he that poet Lord Byron even composed an early advertising jingle:

'And men unpracticed in exchanging knocks
Must go to Jackson, ere they dare to box.'

Jackson was followed by a quartet of Bristol men: Jem Belcher, Henry Pearce, John Gully and Tom Cribb, all of whom enjoyed a spell as the country's top prize-fighter. Cribb was the man in possession when, in 1811, British boxing gained an international dimension. Black American Tom Molineaux twice challenged the Bristolian for his crown, but retired defeated. Boxing, too, was to admit defeat, albeit temporarily, as the Victorian era and its associated morality frowned on such a barbaric spectacle.

In order to counteract this wave of disapproval, boxing looked to its public relations for the first of many times in its history. The London Prize Ring Rules of 1838, framed by the British Pugilists' Protective Association, were at that time the biggest civilising influence on the sport, and intent on giving it a better image. They had outlawed such previously acceptable practices as kicking, butting and gouging, while boxers who threw themselves to the canvas without being struck now rendered themselves in danger of disqualification.

The first fight in American history had taken place in 1816 between Jacob Hyer and Tom Beasley, but the sport had failed to catch on. An influx of Irishmen, however, fuelled the flame, and boxing became the focus for a rivalry between two camps: the pro-Catholic Tammany Hall faction, and the so-called Native Americans. A challenge match between the two saw Tom Hyer (Jacob's son) and James 'Yankee' Sullivan do battle. Hyer won, but his challenge to William Perry, the English champ went unheeded and he retired at the very top.

Yankee Sullivan as he was when he challenged Hyer in 1849. Sullivan was knocked out in the 16th; Tom Hyer won $5,000 and the American title.

John Morrissey and John Heenan were the pretenders to his throne, and though Heenan, a New York boy, failed to beat his wily opponent thanks to breaking four fingers on the corner post, he succeeded to the title when Morrissey — known as 'Old Smoke' because of a badly scarred back — retired.

John L. Sullivan after downing an opponent.

And Heenan it was who crossed the Atlantic in 1860 to make history as one of the contestants in the last great prizefight ever to be staged in England. It took place at Farnborough, Hampshire, and his opponent was English champion Tom Sayers. Sayers was a big man in spirit, but lacked somewhat in stature, standing just 5ft 8in tall, six inches shy of his well-muscled opponent. Their clash was billed as the championship of the world, and the assembled multitude ranged in social stature from Lords and Members of Parliament to the denizens of London's underworld out for a day in the country.

Unlike most world championships since, this one started at the very early hour of 7.30am, and had point-scoring been in operation the American challenger would undoubtedly have walked it. Having hit the deck on numerous occasions in the first five rounds, Sayers then sustained a broken arm — yet incredibly, by clever tactics, he managed to close the American's right eye. As one-armed champion clinched with one-eyed challenger in the 36th, the ring collapsed and a draw declared. Both would be awarded belts for their part in an epic. The big match had ended unresolved, but the focus of attention was about to switch — with irrevocable effect — to the United States.

The 12 Queensberry Rules, that would henceforth govern boxing, were put together by John Graham Chambers, a graduate of Cambridge University, who persuaded Queensberry, a keen amateur, to led them his name and thus a sense of authority. The major innovation stated that the ring should be 24ft square, or 'as near as practicable', while rounds were each to be of three minutes, with a one-minute break. Gloves were also now mandatory.

Many of the rules have since been amended, sometimes due to feelings within the sport and other times in an attempt

The Queensberry Rules, Published in 1867 were as follows:

1. To be a fair stand-up boxing match in a 24-foot ring, or as near that size as practicable.
2. No wrestling or hugging allowed.
3. The rounds of three minutes' duration and one minute time between rounds.
4. If either man fall through weakness or otherwise, he must get up unassisted, 10 seconds to be allowed him to do so, the other man meanwhile to return to his corner; and when the fallen man is on his legs the round to be resumed and continued till the three minutes have expired. If one man fails to come to the scratch in the 10 seconds allowed, it shall be in the power of the referee to give his award in the favour of the other man.
5. A man hanging on the ropes in a helpless state, with his toes off the ground, shall be considered down.
6. No seconds or any other person to be allowed in the ring during the rounds.
7. Should the contest be stopped by any unavoidable interference, the referee to name the time and place as soon as possible for finishing the contest, so that the match must be won and lost unless the backers of the men agree to draw the stakes.
8. The gloves to be fair-sized boxing gloves of the best quality and new.
9. Should the glove burst, or come off, it must be replaced to the referee's satisfaction.
10. A man on one knee is considered down, and if struck is entitled to the stakes.
11. No shoes or boots with springs allowed.
12. The contest in all other respects to be governed by the revised rules of the London Prize Ring.

The 8th Marquis of Queensbury, whose rules boxing still follows today.

to improve safety. Since 1963, for instance, there have been no more 'saved by the bell' decisions, while the following year saw the introduction of the standing eight-count, which the referee can give any boxer who, though still on his feet, seems to be in difficulties. Such changes may have altered the face of boxing, but the impact of the original dozen Rules in helping regulate the sport and giving it credibility cannot be underestimated.

The career of John L. Sullivan bestrode the bare-knuckle and gloved eras of boxing. In February 1882, he became the last bare-knuckle heavyweight champion by beating Paddy Ryan in nine rounds, while seven years later — having meanwhile drawn with Briton Charlie Mitchell — he took a 'mere' 75 rounds (2hr 15min) to vanquish Jake Kilrain in what was to be the last bare-knuckle title fight. Both were in fact prosecuted after it for breaking Mississippi state laws, but neither served their time. It was, however, time for boxing to 'go legit'.

Sullivan therefore donned leather in September 1892 to face James J. 'Gentleman Jim' Corbett in what would generally be considered the first gloved heavyweight title fight. (Some archivists suggest Frank Slavin of Australia won the honour the previous year, fighting Jake Kilrain in 4oz gloves.) Sullivan's 21-round defeat — the first he'd suffered in 45 contests — brought an era to a symbolic end. Corbett's fast-jabbing style would be recognised as boxing today, while Sullivan's wild blows belonged to a previous generation. He'd also declined to fight black men, a decision that not only excluded many potential challengers but, in retrospect, renders his proud boast, 'I can lick any son-of-a-bitch in the house', a trifle hollow.

Corbett was a former bank clerk who'd emerged from San Francisco to challenge for the championship. He fought the first American contest under the Queensberry Rules against Australian champ Peter Jackson; though declared a draw after 61 rounds, Corbett had gained kudos having fought a man Sullivan had refused to fight — albeit on grounds of race.

Five years later, Corbett would fall in the 14th round to Bob Fitzsimmons, a man who can claim the honour of being the first English-born world heavyweight champion. He'd already made history by lifting the crown of 'Nonpareil' Jack Dempsey, the first middleweight champion, before moving up in weight to the top division.

He knocked out Sullivan's conqueror in the 14th round of a fight that made history by being the first title bout to be filmed. Ironically, Corbett had been a guinea-pig for the first ever filmed fight, an exhibition held in Thomas Alva Edison's studio. He won that one — but then that had been scripted . . .

The success of the film, which was shown successfully throughout the world, proved the potential which television would later pick up on. Not only did legal and pirated copies circulate, but there had also apparently been a fake made with actors playing the part of victor and vanquished.

As well as making film history, the year of 1897 would be remembered for the first world championship bout to end in tragedy: Walter Croot was the victim, hitting his head after being knocked out by bantamweight Jimmy Barry at London's National Sporting Club.

James J. Jeffries was a former sparring partner of 'Gentleman Jim' Corbett but lacked any of his ring companion's style. He not only revenged Corbett's defeat against Fitzsimmons when they met in June 1899 but once won, he defended his title for a full five years. Among his defences was the very first world heavyweight championship to be decided on a points decision, against Tom Sharkey in November 1899. He would eventually retire undefeated, handing his title to Marvin Hart.

Hart was beaten in his very first defence by Canadian-born Tommy Burns, real name Noah Brusso, who travelled the world defending his title until appropriately, on Boxing Day 1908, Jack Johnson tracked him down to Rushcutter's Bay, Sydney, and took the crown back home from Australia to the States.

Johnson's win not only made him a household name, it was also historic in making him the first black man to have earned boxing's ultimate accolade. This provoked mixed reactions in a nation still very much divided on racial lines, and disgraceful scenes ensued in certain states as a result of this win. As tension subsided, a 'Great White Hope' was sought to unseat the champion — but James J. Jeffries, who returned from retirement in an ill-advised bid to claim the crown he'd given away, failed to finish the job in July 1910.

Johnson, meanwhile, would become a controversial champion. Out of the ring, he lived a high-rollers lifestyle, while three marriages to white women and his stature as a Chicago night-club owner were enough to put white middle-class sensitivities out of joint. He was made an example of when he violated the newly-passed Mann Act, an obscure piece of legislation designed to stop women from being taken across state lines for immoral purposes. Years later Chuck Berry would be hit by the self-same petard — but while the rock'n'roller served his time, albeit unwillingly, Johnson skipped bail and, after failing to draw the crowds in Europe, ended up in Cuban exile.

He still had his title belt in his well-worn luggage, however, and was persuaded to defend it for the sixth time against the giant Jess Willard, a former rodeo-rider and cowherd from Kansas. The odds were all on Johnson in the 100°F-plus Havana heat — but the 26th round would see referee Jack Welsh raise the challenger's arm aloft. In retrospect, it wasn't a shock win: Johnson, now 37, had been out of training and over-confident. Yet in his prime he'd been the greatest — some say of all time.

Back in Britain, boxing was on its way back. And the Lonsdale Belt, instituted by

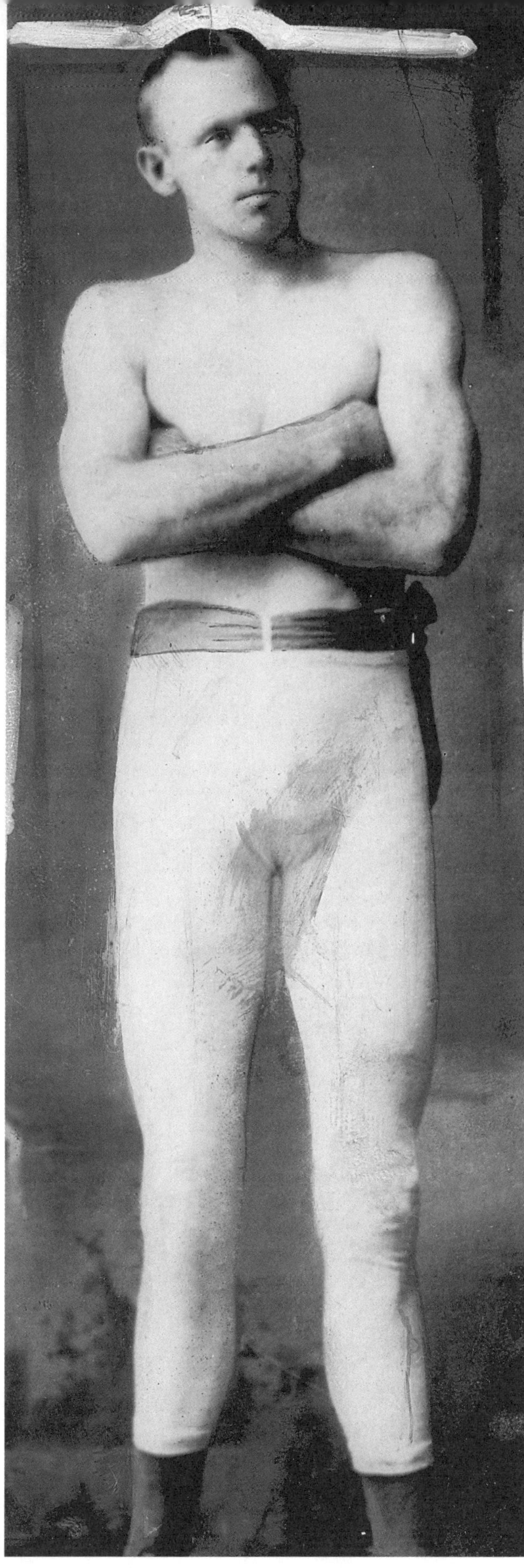

Helston-born Bob Fitzsimmons became champion in 1897 when he defeated James J. Corbett.

the National Sporting Club in 1909, was to prove the emerging sport's ultimate status symbol. The first recipient was Freddie Welsh, who had attained the prerequisite of winning three times at a given weight.

The belts were originally solid gold, but though they became gold-plated later on were equally prized by British boxers. The only American to win a belt was Joe Louis, this marking his defence against Briton Tommy Farr.

Boxing had first featured in the Olympic programme at St Louis in 1904, though it was absent eight years later in Sweden where the sport was banned! The intervening year had been so poorly patronised the entire programme had taken just a day to complete! World War I then called a halt, but boxing was on the agenda from 1920 onwards and rapidly became one of the games' main events.

The path from Olympic medal to the clink of gold coins would become a well-worn one over the years since flyweight Frankie Genaro followed gold in the first postwar games in 1920 with the NBA world title in 1924. Politics would rear its ugly head over the years — Muhammad Ali cast away his medal, insisting it was 'tainted' by racial prejudice — but the importance of an Olympic title to channel young hopefuls into the sport was generally appreciated.

The period following the First World War would, in retrospect, be regarded as something of a golden age for the sport. America as ever led the way, and 1920 would see the New York State Athletic Commission and the newly-formed National Boxing Association flex their muscles as the sport got its organisational act together.

Leading the way in the ring was Jack Dempsey, the sport's first postwar superhero (not to be confused with 19th century middleweight 'Nonpareil' Jack Dempsey). A country at peace yet uneasy with itself identified with a man who, in the words of one critic, was 'Red Grange, Babe Ruth, Al Jolson, Paavo Nurmi and Man O'War rolled into one.' Quite a billing, but one Jack did his best to live up to.

Legend has it Dempsey's mother read her baby John L Sullivan's biography, having bought it from a travelling salesman at her doorstep: true or not, it added to the legend which Dempsey himself took little time in polishing to an impressive lustre. The Colorado-born champion to be was earning a living in a local silvermine, aged just 15, when he first used his fists in anger. His brother Bernie had been fighting under the name Jack Dempsey, but one night had to pull out of a bout. His brother, born William Harrison Dempsey, was only too eager to deputise, and liked the name so much he kept it!

Having moved to the West Coast to work in the shipbuilding industry, Dempsey found a manager when he intervened in a bar-room brawl. The man whose odds he evened, one Jack Kearns,

Jack Dempsey, the 'Manassa Mauler', whose fight with Georges Carpentier was the first to be worth more than £1 million. He died in 1983.

Gene Tunny beating Jack Dempsey in the championship fight for the world heavyweight title before a 150,000 crowd in Chicago in 1929. Tunny defeated Dempsey on points, but the fight will be remembered for the controversial long count caused by Dempsey's refusal to go to a neutral corner, after crashing Tunney to the canvas in the 7th round.

was so impressed by the ring skills of the man who saved his bacon he offered to enter a partnership with him if he returned to full-time pugilism.

It was an invitation that opened a record-breaking sequence of 26 fights won in the first round over his first four years of boxing. Dempsey's route to the top left him one major hurdle — Jess Willard, the Kansas Giant who stood atop the pile with little real competition. When they met in Toledo in June 1919, it was all over for him after just three round as he threw in the towel, leaving the Manassa Mauler undisputed champion.

Having beaten an opponent five inches taller and some 65lb heavier, Dempsey was clearly a leading light as the sport gathered momentum. He became the first boxer to draw million-dollar-plus receipts when beating European champ Georges Carpentier in July 1921. Carpentier, a national hero in France who'd won titles at every weight, had something to do with it too. But he was knocked out in four rounds in what was, incidentally, the first world championship bout to be broadcast live on the radio.

The charismatic Carpentier, with his film star looks, was the first of a string of light-heavyweights (the class established in the early days of the 20th century by Lou Houseman, a Chicago newspaperman) who'd move up to the top division, but none would prove successful until Michael Spinks cracked it in 1985.

Someone who would prove as influential out of the ring as Dempsey did in it was promoter Tex Rickard. Having promoted his first fight in 1906 between Joe Gans and Battling Nelson, he'd go on to stage over 230 fights before his death in 1929. Four years before that, he'd built his lasting legacy to boxing in the shape of Madison Square Garden, New York's premier indoor sporting arena situated on 49th Street and 8th Avenue.

Rickard was the first of boxing's many major-league promoters. Though few would leave such a visible legacy, all would play a major part in bringing boxing to the fore as a major sport. Rickard had been a professional gambler before moving into the fight game — and while he'd been fortunate in having Dempsey at his disposal, he proved over time that his hunches were worth backing.

Dempsey's reign ended in September 1925 when Gene Tunney proved too skilful an opponent. In truth, the champ found himself an ex-champ as much for the reason that he'd taken a two-year 'holiday' to begin a movie career alongside his wife, screen star Estelle Taylor. His riposte to her when she asked what went wrong — 'Honey, I forgot to duck' — would go down in ring history.

A rematch on the last day of 1927 brought a similar result, but was also to go down in history as the night of the 'long count'. Dempsey, having floored his opponent, seemingly refused to go to the neutral corner and let Tunney take the count. By the time the referee, one Dave Barry, had persuaded him to do so and restarted the count, Tunney had regained his wits . . . and ultimately retained his title. He retired undefeated after what would be Tex Rickard's last promotion.

Then came the long, dark days of the American Depression. Few fighters of the era had the charisma necessary to persuade Americans to part with their distinctly limited supply of dollars, the likes of Jack Sharkey and German Max Schmeling leading a decidedly piecemeal field. The pair's Yankee Stadium meeting in June 1970 grossed $700,000, exceptional for the time, but the fight was decided by a controversial foul punch.

Italian giant Primo Carnera was the next contender — and what a contender, at over 6ft 5in and some 270lb. Yet his alleged connection to the Mafia combined with his ungainly appearance to render him a less than credible champion. His defeat by high-living Max Baer in 1934 was generally welcomed.

The biggest news of the prewar period was made in 1938 by Mississippi-born Henry Armstrong who, for four months, achieved an unthinkable feat by topping three weights at world level. On defeating Lou Ambers on points, 'Hurricane Hank' added the lightweight crown to the featherweight and welterweight he'd already won. What was more he'd go on to mount a middleweight title challenge with

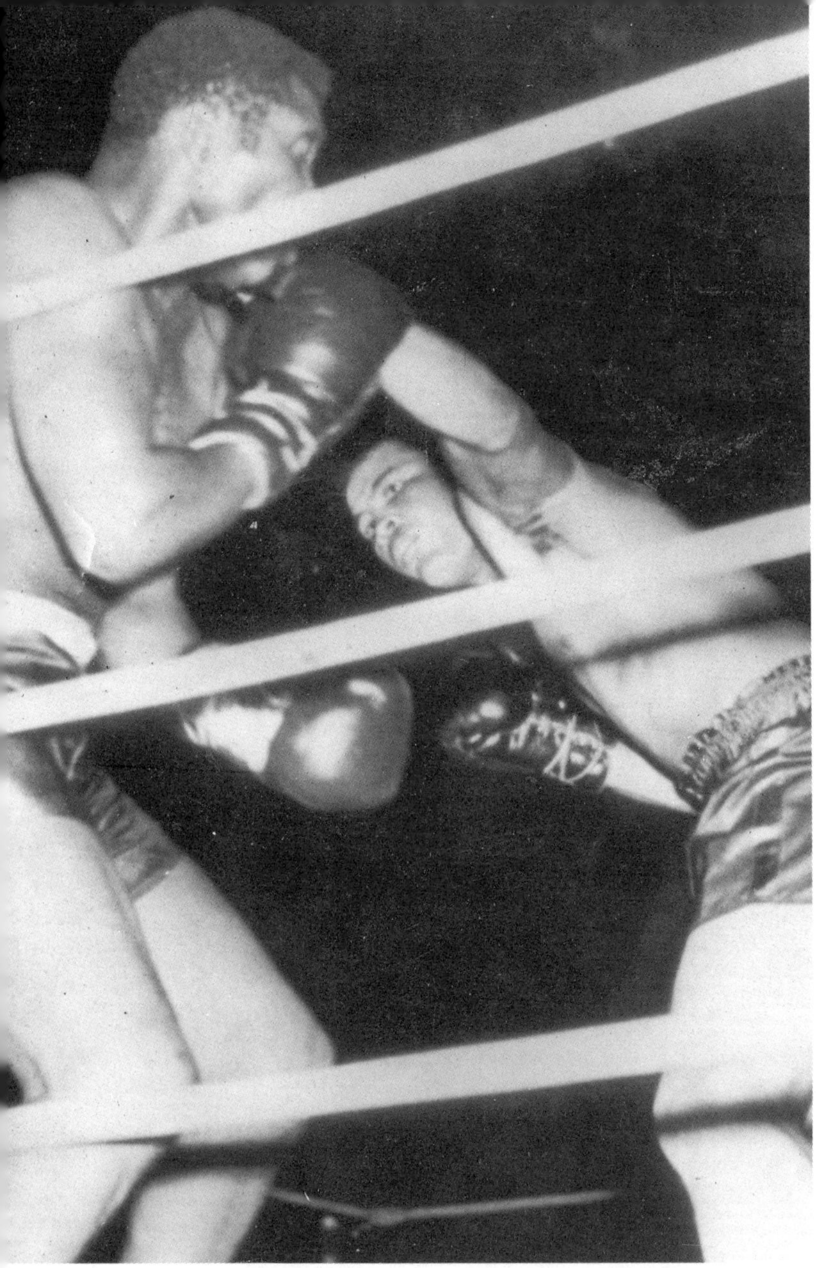

Joe Louis putting in a powerful left to the chin of Sugar Ray Robinson, when making his comeback in the ring after being discharged from the army. The exhibition bout was held in the Civic Auditorium, San Francisco on 16 November 1945.

Ceferino Garcia in 1940, but could only draw. Perhaps it was the power of prayer that fuelled him, because he became a Baptist minister after retiring in 1945.

If the reign of Jack Johnson had emphasised America's continuing racial divide, then Joe Louis was a fighter whose dignity and example would unite and inspire a nation. His death in 1981 was not only mourned nationally, but he was accorded the honour of burial in the Arlington National Cemetery, the resting place of national heroes and legends.

Born Joe Louis Barrow in prejudice-torn Alabama in 1914, legend has it he spent the money his mother gave him for music lessons on boxing tuition, and by 20 had turned professional and started an impressive run of performances that would take him to the very top. Mike Jacobs, a former Big Apple ticket scalper, was Louis's promoter and the pair proved a perfect combination.

Louis's record of 63 wins in 66 contests tells only part if the story. An early set-back at the experienced hands of Max Schmeling in 1934 was a blow — but 25 successful defences of his world title after beating Jim Braddock (the man who'd beaten Max Baer) in June 1937 is undoubtedly impressive. He would have retired undefeated, too, but returned to pay tax debts and found he'd pushed himself one fight too many. Defeats to Ezzard Charles and Rocky Marciano in 1950 and 1951 ended his career on an unfortunate note, but President Kennedy ordered his tax bill to be written off while Las Vegas's Caesar's Palace venue were happy to employ one of America's living legends until ill-health took its toll.

Louis's fight landmarks, and there were many, included the last scheduled 20-round world title fight with Bob Pastor in September 1939 and perhaps his best ever victory two years later when he knocked out Billy Conn in the 13th round to retain the heavyweight title despite trailing on points.

As Louis bowed out, his victor

Floyd Patterson put paid to Henry Cooper's hopes after only 2min 20sec at Wembley in September 1966. The British and Empire champion took a count of nine before Patterson loosed a rapid left and right which sent Cooper to the canvas out cold.

Marciano weighed in — but he was a more unlikely champion, standing two inches short of six feet and not having entered the professional fight game until well into his twenties. Yet unlike Joe Louis, he enjoyed the luxury of retiring undefeated with a perfect record. Reports differ as to why he didn't make it a round half-century, one being that he'd damaged his back while playing with his baby daughter at home. Whatever the facts, 49 wins and no defeats remained a proud record.

The beneficiary of his decision was Floyd Patterson who, when knocking out Archie Moore in 1956, would become the youngest ever world heavyweight champ. Patterson would lose, then regain, then lose the title again — a pattern not untypical of the heavyweight scene at that time.

In other weights, Britain had gained a champion in the shape of Freddie Mills — the first in a line of promising but ultimately limited postwar heroes that would include Henry Cooper, Joe Bugner and most recently Frank Bruno. Victory against Gus Lesnevich after 15 action-

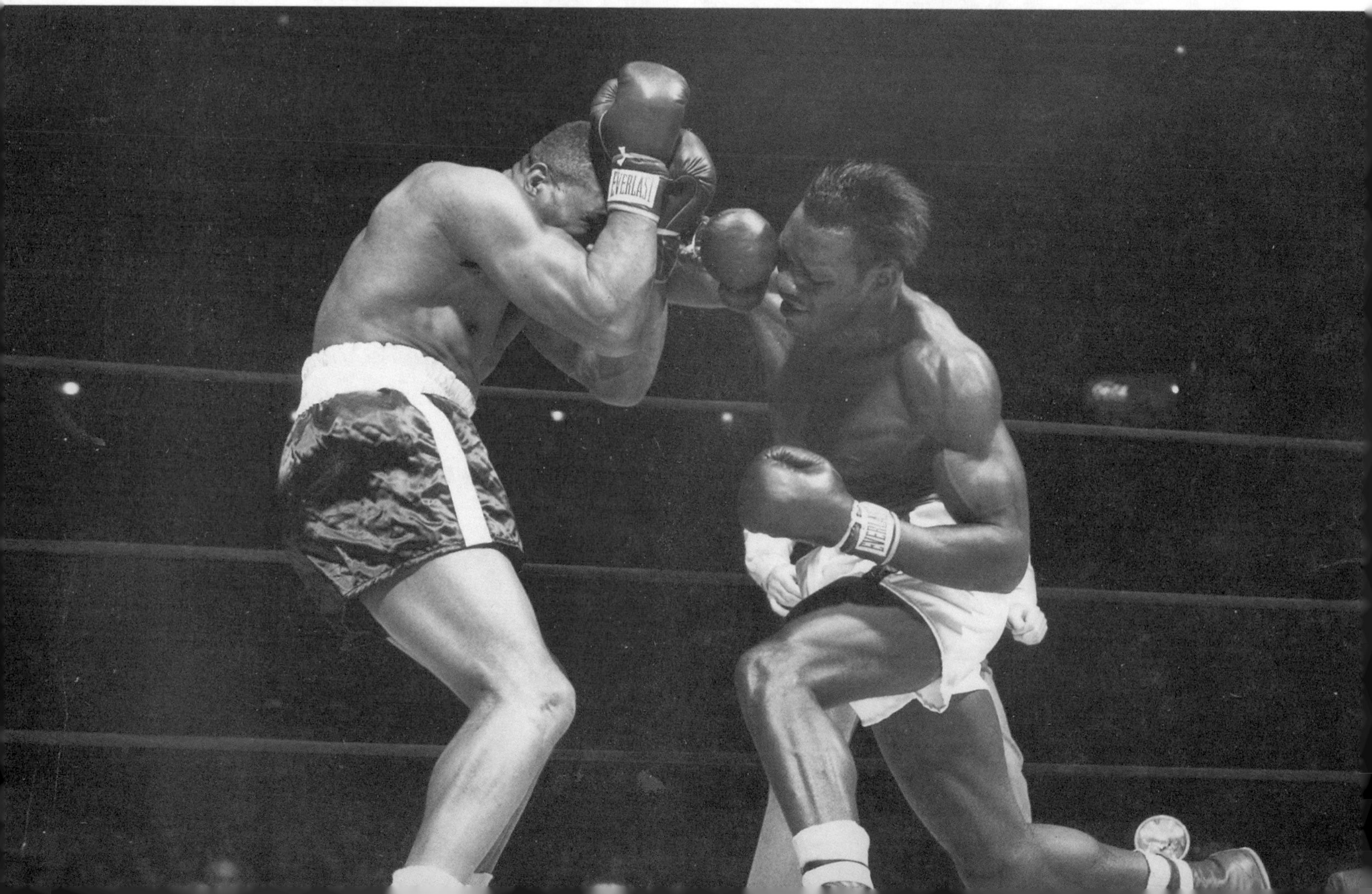
EVERLAST
EVERLAST

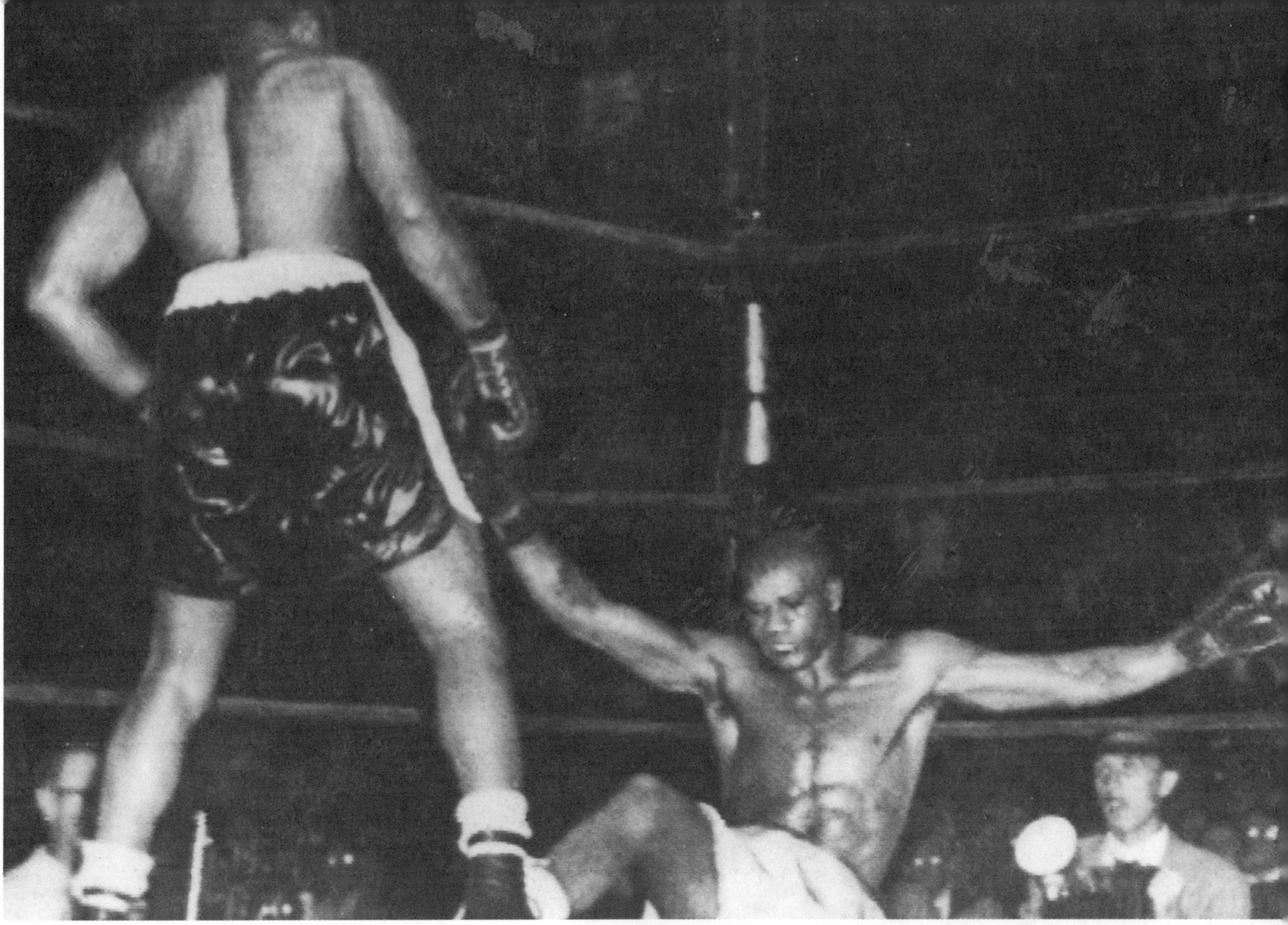

Scenes from the 1950s:

ABOVE LEFT: Floyd Patterson won gold at the 1952 Helsinki Olympics — at middleweight. Renowned for his speed and combination punching, he beat Archie Moore for the vacant heavyweight title; he lost and regained the title against Ingamar Johanssen before losing it for good to 'Sonny' Liston in 1962. He is seen here beating Tommy Jackson in 1957.

BELOW LEFT: In 1951 Jersey Joe Walcott knocked out Izzard Charles to become the oldest heavyweight champion. His reign was not long — Marciano beat him in 1952. He is seen during his 1950 fight against Omelio Agramonte (right).

ABOVE: Archie Moore was the world light heavyweight champion from 1955 for nine years. He lost to Floyd Patterson when trying for the vacant heavyweight crown. Here he stops Harold Johnson in 1954.

RIGHT: Joe Louis (left) out on his feet against Izzard Charles in September 1950. Charles beat Jersey Joe Walcott in 1948 for the vacant championship but would lose to the same opponent later in the year.

him, Pep continued in the ring until within sight of his 40th birthday, clocking up an amazing 242 fights, and came back in the mid-1960s when well past his prime.

One of Pep's two defeats as an amateur had been against Ray Robinson (real name Walker Smith), who'd go on to the first great middleweight of the postwar era. 'Sugar Ray' had already been the world's top welterweight for four years when he moved up to win the first of five middleweight titles in February 1951, stopping Jake LaMotta in 14 rounds. That Valentine's Day win continued a love affair with his public that even survived Briton Randolph Turpin taking his crown in July. A September rematch saw Sugar Ray reconfirmed as world champ after a 64-day hiatus. He'd lose only 19 of 201 professional fights and was never knocked out.

He moved up again to light-heavyweight in 1952 to challenge Joey Maxim, but in a hot and humid encounter at Yankee Stadium — so hot the referee had

packed rounds in July 1948 gave him a brief spell as undisputed world light-heavyweight champ.

Born Guglielmo Papaleo, Willie Pep earned another nickname — that of 'Will o' the Wisp' — during his reign as featherweight champion. Interestingly, another top featherweight Bal Battalino had emerged from Connecticut before him: perhaps it was something in the water. Pep's world reign between 1946 and 1950 was interrupted by a defeat by arch-rival Sandy Saddler, from whom he regained his crown in a rematch four months later. Though Saddler later got the better of

ABOVE: Randolph Turpin, middleweight champion of the world in 1951 after besting Sugar Ray Robinson in a memorable encounter.

RIGHT: Ingemar Johannson, the European heavyweight champion, in a publicity shot taken while preparing to defend his title against Joe Erskine, the British champion, on 21 February 1958 in Göteborg, Sweden.

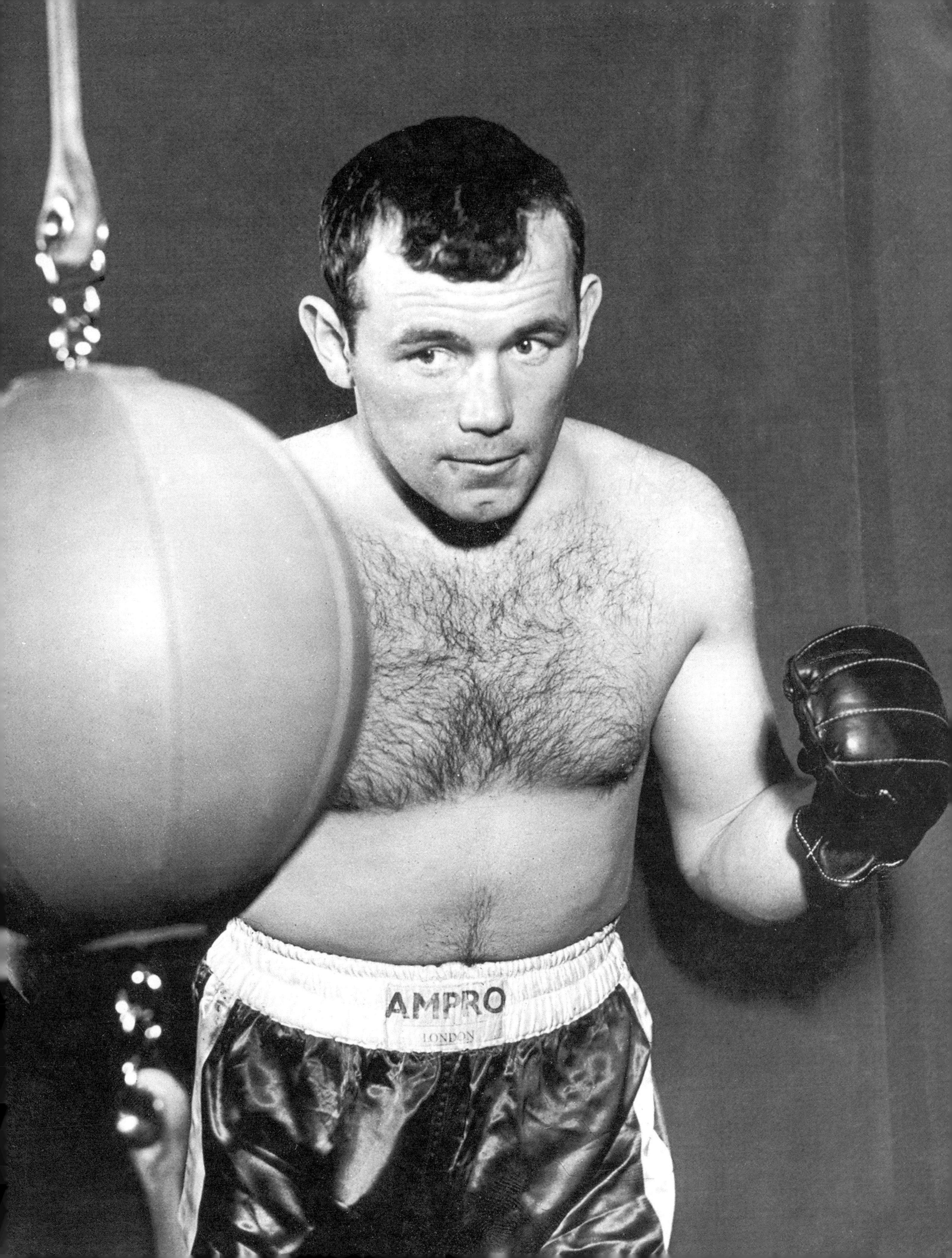
AMPRO
LONDON

The young and hungry Muhammed Ali in England preparing to fight Brian London for the world heavyweight title at Earl's Court in August 1966. Muhammed's trainer, Angelo Dundee, confidently predicted the end result — a knock out victory for the champion.

to retire — he failed to come out for the 14th despite being ahead on points. It was his first defeat for nine years. Robinson enjoyed the well-earned fruits of his success with conspicuous symbols like a pink Cadillac, but unlike say Jack Johnson he was universally liked and respected and his death in 1989 brought fulsome tributes from all quarters.

There were few big names around to enliven boxing at the end of the 1950s; Davey Moore made the featherweight division his own from 1959, but would be remembered for his tragic death days after being relieved of the world title by Cuban Sugar Ramos. The heavyweight title left the States in 1959 when Ingemar Johansson returned home to Sweden after stopping Floyd Patterson in New York. But Patterson became the first man ever to regain the heavyweight title, knocking out Johansson in five rounds the following year.

Patterson defended his title against Sonny Liston against manager Cus D'Amato's advice — and though he lost to the man with a ne'er-do-well image in the first round, the payday of $1,434,000 for their rematch, which Liston also won with similar ease, must have been some consolation. Patterson's conqueror would in turn cede the title to Cassius Clay in February 1964.

Further down the weights, March 1960 saw Gabriel 'Flash' Elorde win the then recently revived super-featherweight title, inactive since Sandy Saddler left it in 1951. Elorde's 10 defences would regain the division general acceptance. But if that was a success story in the making, Joe Brown was establishing a lightweight record in October 1961 by retaining the title for the 11th and final time when he beat Bert Somodio on a points decision. Carlos Ortiz, the Puerto Rican who took over, would rule the division on and off for most of the 1960s

As the National Boxing Association changed its name to become the World Boxing Association in 1962, it instigated the new weight division of light-middleweight (or junior-middleweight, as the Americans preferred to call it) which would remain an undivided championship until 1975. Less welcome to the WBA was the 1963 formation of the World Boxing Council, which despite the weight of history being against it would go on to become the most influential of the so-called 'Alphabet Boys' attempting to control the sport of boxing.

The WBC, for instance, would be the organisation to take the number of rounds in world championship fights down from the standard 15 to 12 in 1982 — a decision later taken on board all-round. And with José Dulaiman at the helm, the WBC would prove a major player in the fight game.

Just as Rocky Marciano had brought Italian-Americans to boxing, so Cassius Clay would become the role model for black youth throughout the United States. Along with soul singer James Brown and civil rights leader Martin Luther King, he'd prove one of the most important black Americans of a generation.

A group of far-sighted businessman saw enough when Clay returned from the Rome Olympics with a gold medal that they agreed to bankroll his professional career. Purses would be shared 50-50, with Clay — then on the generous salary of $400 per month — matched with trainer

ABOVE: Mayhem as referee Jersey Joe Walcott pushes a snarling Cassius Clay away from Sonny Liston after a knockout in the first round in May 1965.

Angelo Dundee. The raw material Dundee had to work with was immense: 6ft 3in and 200lb, Ali was blessed with all the physical attributes and more. He also proved a worthy first champion of the television age, with soundbite potential a-plenty.

His proud boasts of when his opponent would hit the canvas made him headline news, even when the predictions proved less than accurate; while slogans like 'float like a butterfly, sting like a bee' made back in 1964 are still in common parlance today.

The advent of television had brought boxing in general — and Clay in particular — into millions of living rooms worldwide, boosting the sport beyond measure and making its superstars household names the world over. The first fight to be shown on TV had been screened live as long ago as 4 April 1938, and involved Len Harvey and Jock McAvoy, while the bout between Max Baer and Lou Nova in June 1939 had led to predictions that the innovation would change the face of the sport. The advent of war had stopped the show, of course, but it was no coincidence that the arrival of TV in the world's households in the 1950s and 1960s would give boxing its highest profile yet.

Clay renounced his 'slave name' and on converting to the Muslim religion became Muhammad Ali. Resisting the draft ('I ain't got no quarrel with them Viet Kongs') took his title where opponents had failed — yet unlike Jack Johnson before him Ali refused to run. Three years off seemed to do him no harm at all, however, and he returned to set up what was, on 8 March 1971, billed as the 'Fight of the Champions'. Ali was set to face 'Smokin' Joe Frazier, the man who'd prospered in his absence to emerge at the top of the heavyweight pile.

There would be no losers in this bout — a split $5 million purse would see to that — but considerable pride was at stake as the once and current champions did battle. And it was Frazier who emerged triumphant, the outcome decided even before his 12th-round knockout punch. It wasn't the end of the matter, though, as the two biggest heavyweights of the TV age were called upon to stage a repeat performance.

George Foreman, though, had other ideas — and by jolting Joe in Jamaica in early 1973 he conclusively derailed the Ali-Frazier bandwagon. As it turned out, the rematch would be for the right to fight Foreman, but the absence of a belt hanging on the outcome didn't matter. Indeed Ali had lost to Ken Norton en route.

The rematch in January 1974 at Madison Square Garden squared the series. Ali never looked in trouble and might have finished the fight in the second but for referee Tony Perez hearing imaginary bells and ending the round early. 'You was much better than I thought,' he later told his opponent, magnanimous in victory as ever. Foreman having demolished Ken Norton, Ali now had another challenge to face.

Muhammed Ali out for revenge against Ken Norton who had humiliated him six months earlier. Ali won on points on a split decision.

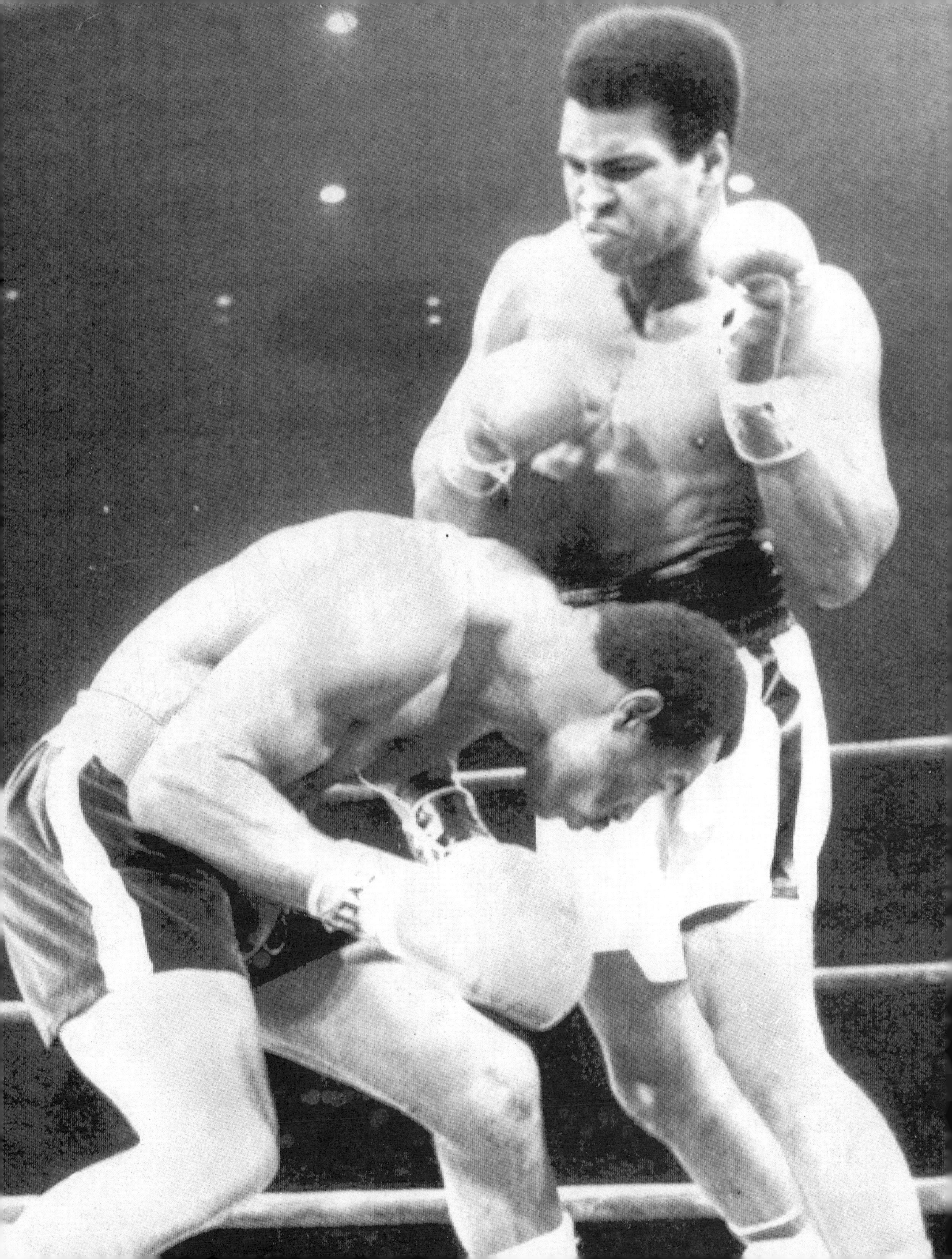

As Cassius Clay or Muhammed Ali, the self-proclaimed 'Greatest' bestrode the world of boxing from the early 1960s until well into the 1970s, his third spell as world champion starting as late as 1978. While his latterday record may show resilience and grit, his early years were characterised by a supreme mix of speed, technique and power. TOP: Fighting Floyd Patterson in 1965. ABOVE: Against 'Sonny' Liston. RIGHT: Hamming for the crowd against Richard Dunn in 1976. FAR RIGHT: Fighting Brian London in 1966.

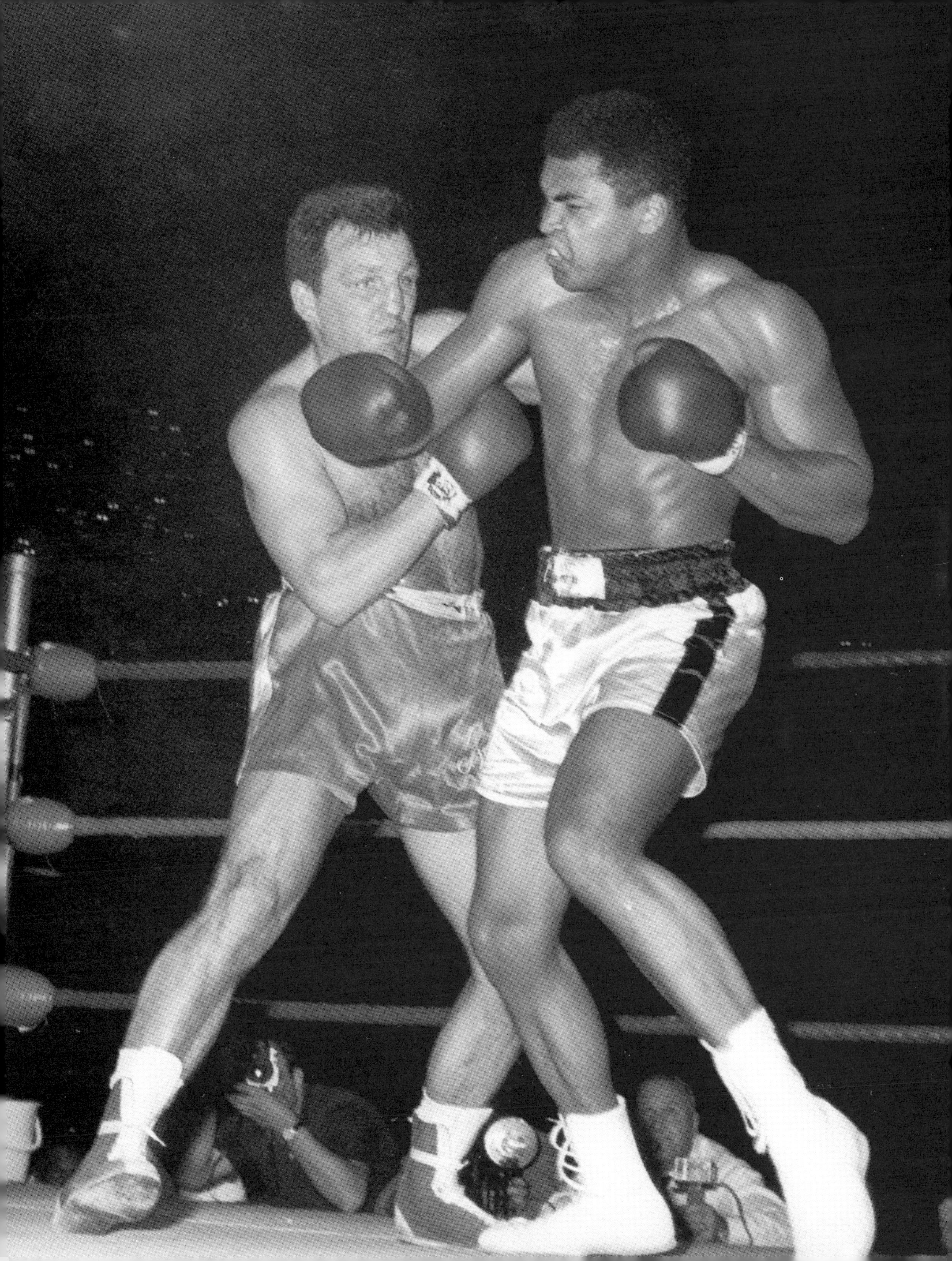

In July 1973 Joe Frazier beat Joe Bugner on points at Earls Court. At the time Bugner was the 23-year old European champion, and Frazier was hungry to get the chance to regain his world title which he had lost to George Foreman in January in Jamaica. Foreman was ringside to assess his progress.

The showdown was in the African country of Zaire, formerly the Belgian Congo, the showdown promoted by Don King, a man who, having put himself on the map with this epic confrontation, would soon become legendary in the fight game. The location had been the choice of a Swiss company that had partially financed the match.

Ali, who'd typically promised to 'float' like a butterfly, sting like a bee' made none of the running, but said he'd take Foreman in eight. The 'Rumble in the Jungle' ended in success for Ali, while Foreman, who'd later make boxing history by coming back at the age of 38 and taking a world title eight years later, would retire to become a minister of religion.

Ali faced Frazier again the following year in the third fight between the giants was dubbed the 'Thriller In Manila' by an ever-hungry press. It was stopped despite Frazier's protests.

Ali's first fight with Frazier in New York in March 1971 had opened a new era for televised boxing. Critics had argued for some time that the sport had been selling itself too cheaply, and certainly Gillette's Fight Of The Week, boxing's earliest showcase that had been screened for two decades to 1964, had run its course. The take-up of some 1.3 million to watch the world's two top heavyweights do battle on closed-circuit television clearly showed the potential that would be taken up in the age of pay-per-view, when the public would pay for ringside seats in their own living room.

Henry Cooper would not be playing a part in that revolution. The only boxer to win three Lonsdale Belts outright, he retired in 1971 after a controversial defeat on a controversial points verdict against up and coming Joe Bugner. Britain's longest-serving heavyweight champion would retain a great deal of public sympathy not only for the manner of that defeat but his dignity. Bugner, by contrast, was never a big favourite. Having emigrated to extend his career in Australia, he came back in 1987 to fight Frank Bruno in what was the first boxing promotion of snooker supremo Barry Hearn.

Edinburgh-born lightweight champion Ken Buchanan was another Briton to make his mark. Though he was the victim when Roberto Duran won his first world title, taking a beating over 13 rounds in New York, he gave a good account of himself and significantly the Panamanian was never willing to confront him a second time. An attempt at the WBC title ended in failure in 1975, but he won a Lonsdale Belt and many fans during his career.

The year of 1976 saw New York-born Puerto Rican Wilfred Benitez become the youngest world champion in boxing history. He defeated the long-serving WBA light-welterweight champion Antonio Cervantes when aged just 17 years and six months. Sadly a career which promised so much would end in a sad series of comebacks, though he moved up weights to win the WBC welterweight title (1979) and light-middleweight (1981) before personal and management problems struck.

Leon Spinks celebrating winning the heavyweight championship in February 1978. He was given the benefit of a controversial split decision against Muhammed Ali.

The year of Benitez's breakthrough saw boxing receive a shot in the arm, not only through the emergence of three great US fighters at the Montreal Olympics in Ray Leonard and the brothers Leon and Michael Spinks but also the arrival of a celluloid contender. This was Sylvester Stallone, who achieved world fame as Rocky Balboa in what would become an

BRUN

Mirror

ABOVE: Sugar Ray Leonard in pensive mode — and evening dress!

ABOVE RIGHT: Thomas Hearns reaching out a punch at Sugar Ray Leonard during the first round of their super middleweight title fight in Las Vegas in June 1989. The fight ended in a draw.

BELOW RIGHT: 'Marvellous' Marvin Hagler catching one right on the nose from Sugar Ray Leonard. The venue was Las Vegas and the fight a middleweight title bout which Leonard won

PREVIOUS PAGE: Frank Bruno takes on Williams in a 1993 bout.

eponymous and highly successful series of films. After so many years of bad press and the disapproval of the moral majority, it was a welcome morale boost and arguably persuaded a new generation to give the fight game a chance.

Of the Olympic hopefuls, it was Ray Leonard, adopting the 'Sugar' prefix in homage to the great Ray Robinson, who would make the biggest mark after turning pro in 1977, his impact unusual for a welterweight fighter not in the top division. Handsome, articulate and a classy fighter, he was carefully groomed for a shot at the WBC world title. This came in June 1980, and that was where events departed from the script.

He was unfortunate enough to meet a seasoned campaigner in Panama's Roberto Duran, a slugger who'd enjoyed a decade of domination at lightweight but who moved up a division as time took its toll. His waistline may have been thicker, but Duran justified his nickname of manos de piedro or hands of stone by persuading Leonard to forsake his principles and trade blow for blow.

Even in defeat, though, Leonard clearly had star quality — and he rubbed it in Duran's face in the rematch. Duran's inexplicable retirement in the eighth round followed some Ali-like teasing from Leonard, and it was assumed his pride had taken more damage than his body. But while that was the final page of the Duran legend (a junior-middleweight comeback failed), it seemed to be just the start of things for Leonard.

Yet the fight game has a habit of confounding expectations — Sugar Ray enjoyed his third big payday in as many years when he stopped the previously

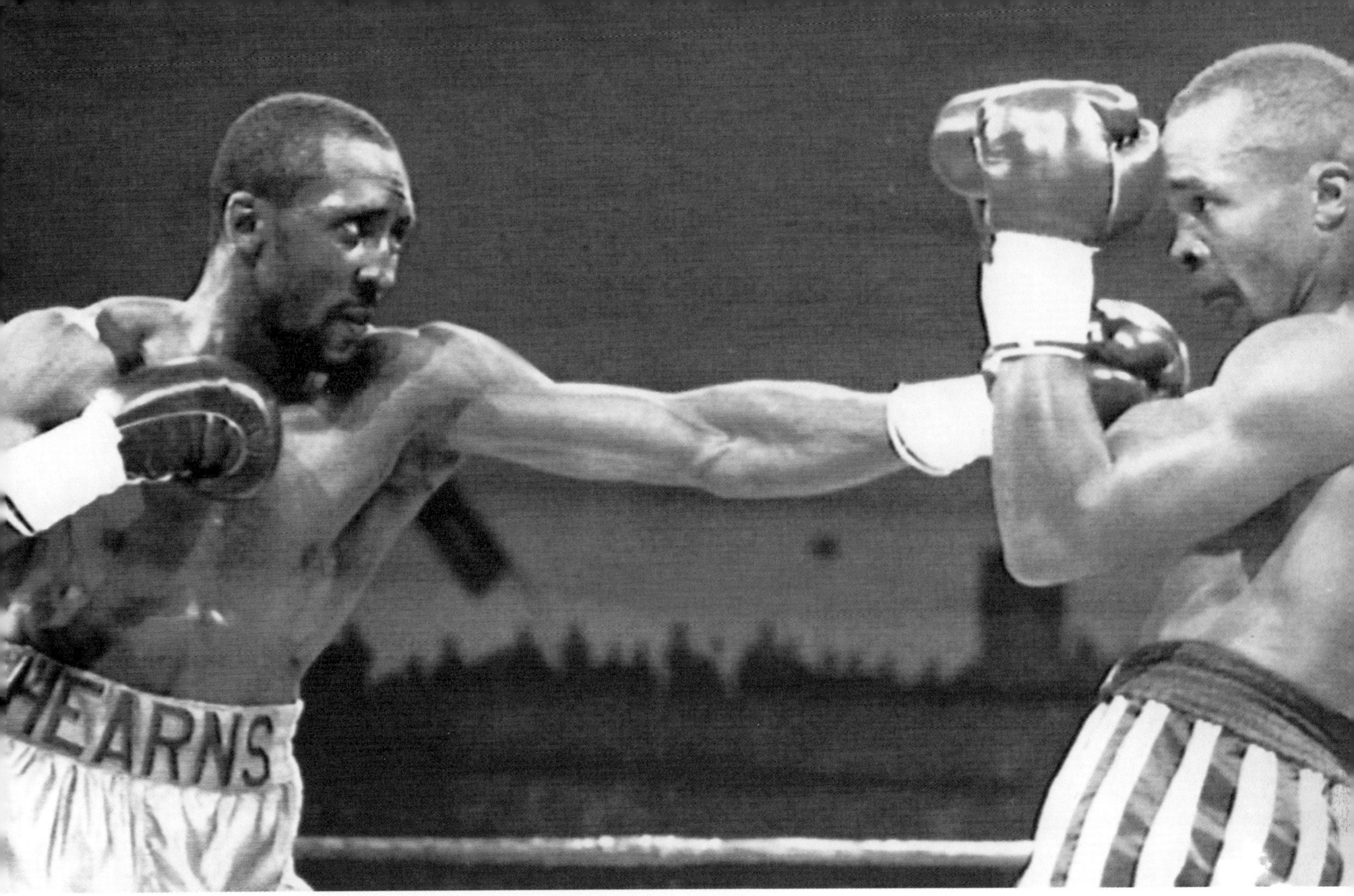
HEARNS

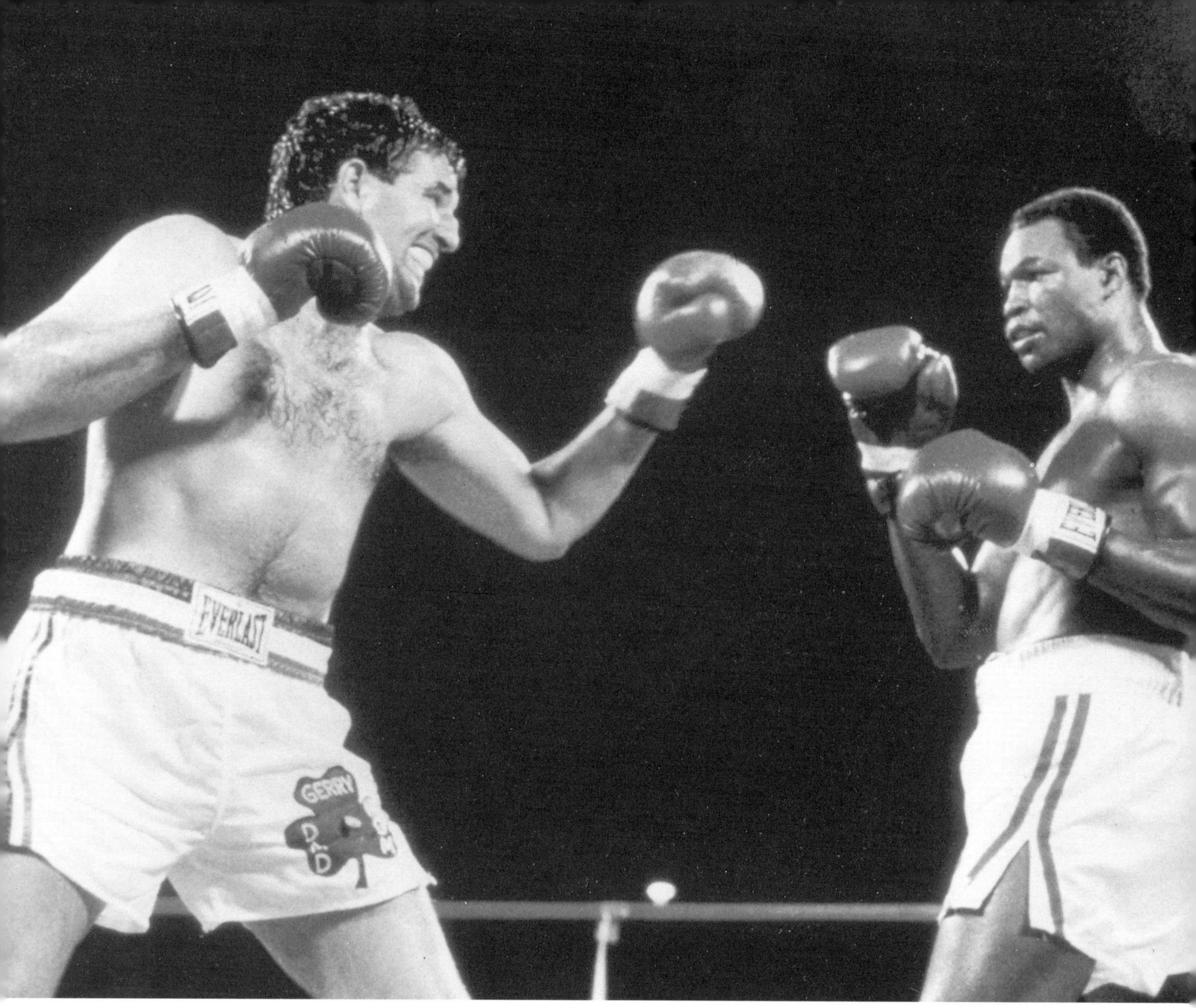

Larry Holmes and Gerry Cooney shaping up to each other. Holmes' 12th title defence was the much-hyped showdown with 'great white hope' Gerry Cooney. This was the most anticipated heavyweight tussle since the Ali–Joe Frazier bouts and ended with the challenger being pulled out of the fight by his corner in the 13th round.

undefeated Thomas 'Hitman' Hearns in September 1981. Victory over Bruce Finch followed, but that he had paid a frightful cost became clear when a detached retina was diagnosed. His retirement was short-lived, but Leonard's return against Kevin Howard proved a one-off . . . for the moment, at least.

Leonard had already achieved much by uniting the world's welterweight titles — a significant feat matched by 'Marvelous' Marvin Hagler in the middleweight division. He proved a worthy successor to the Argentine Carlos Monzon, who'd held the title for most of the 1970s before three years of 'rotating-door' champions. Hagler, distinctive with his shaved head and sinister beard, took the crown against Briton Alan Minter on his home turf at London's Wembley Arena.

Having won the title the hard way, he'd defend it often and vigorously against a stream of quality contenders until, in April 1987, Sugar Ray Leonard was again tempted out of retirement. He ended Hagler's reign after a dozen successful defences on a 12-round points decision, and went on to fight for the WBC light-heavyweight and then the new super-middleweight titles, bidding to be the first fighter to win titles in five divisions (as it turned out, Hearns beat him to the record by just three days). After rematches against Hearns and Duran, Leonard finally came unstuck against Terry Norris.

Argentine ring legend Carlos Monzon also called it a day in 1977, having smashed all middleweight records and become the weight's most successful champion ever. Having beaten Nino Benvenuti in 1970, he made 14 defences against all comers before retiring undefeated. Unfortunately his life outside the ring was nowhere near as successful and, after spending a spell behind bars for killing a girlfriend, he died in a 1995 car crash while out on parole.

The heavyweight roll of honour gained a new and lasting name at the top in June 1978 in the substantial shape of Larry Holmes. The Georgian's victory over Ken Norton not only gave him the WBC heavyweight title but began a 16-fight reign that would last until he relinquished his title in 1983.

His decision to take the new IBF crown rebounded two years after that when Michael Spinks outpointed him — which

Nicaraguan Alexis Arguello ended the reign of Scotland's WBC title holder Jim Watt over a fiercely contested 15 rounds in June 1981.

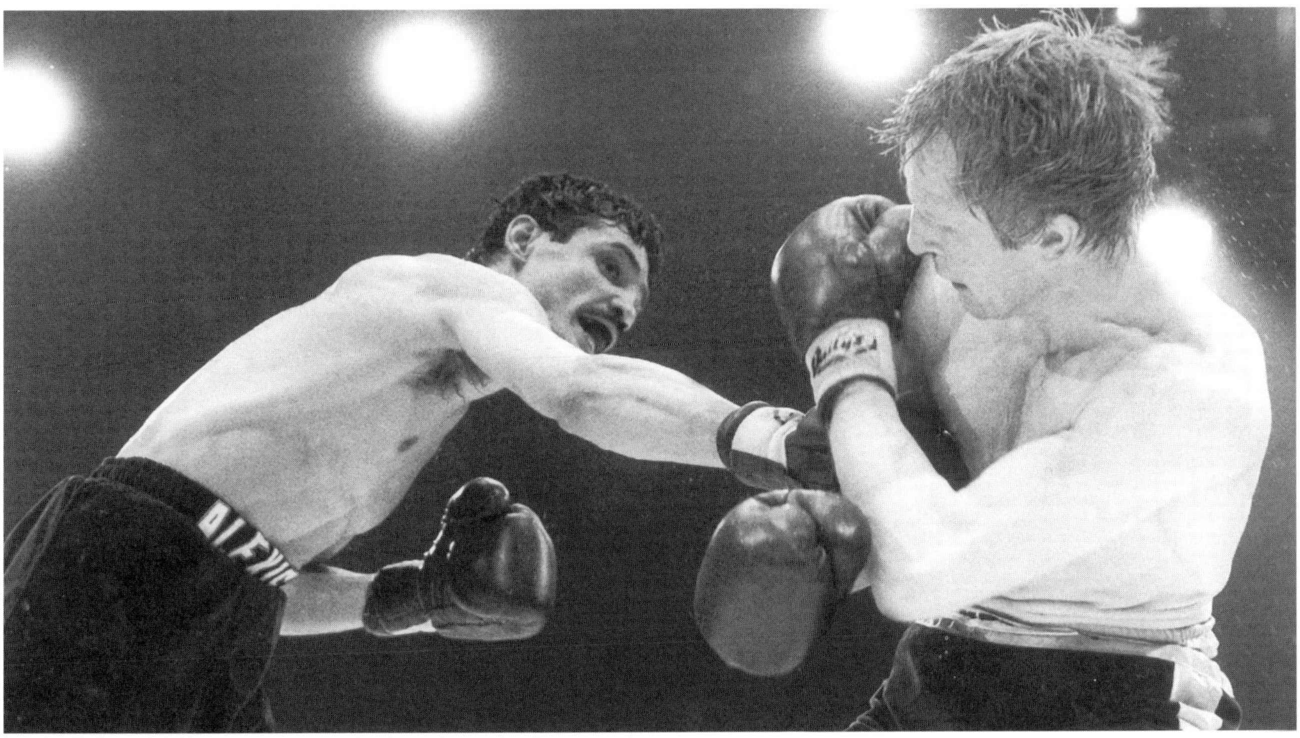

There were giants in those days . . .

The 1970s saw some titanic struggles between powerful heavyweights in a period dominated by the personality of Muhammad Ali.

LEFT: George Foreman won gold at the 1968 Olympics. Having lost to Ali in 1973 he followed his calling to become ordained and returned to boxing a decade later dubbed the 'Punching Preacher'. In 1994 he beat Michael Moorer to become the oldest heavyweight champion and Fighter of the Year.

Here he is seen disposing of Joe Roman in January 1973 (ABOVE LEFT) and Ken Norton in March 1974 (BELOW LEFT).

ABOVE: Larry Holmes was one of Ali's sparring partners. He beat Ken Norton to gain the heavyweight title in 1978. One fight away from beating Rocky Marciano's 49–0 record, in September 1985, he lost to Michael Spinks (right).

RIGHT: Ken Norton had three unforgettable fights against Ali — winning the first (and breaking Ali's jaw) in 1974 and losing the others. Here he disposes of Duane Bobick.

created a certain symmetry, since it had been Leon Spinks' abdication in 1978, when the title was undisputed, that gave Norton the crown which Holmes had snatched. Holmes had started life as Muhammad Ali's sparring partner, and though he fought on into the 1990s, bravely mixing it with Mike Tyson and others, his chance had gone.

Cuban heavyweight Teofilo Stevenson made his mark as perhaps the greatest amateur boxer of all time when in 1980 he won his third Olympic gold at the Moscow Olympics. Cuba forbade its boxers to turn pro and it's said Stevenson turned down a $2 million offer to abide by his and his country's communist principles. Cuba had unsurprisingly dominated the amateur fight game for many years, a state of affairs that was not universally welcomed by the boxing world.

ABOVE: Love him or loathe him, Chris Eubank kept British boxing in the news during his reign as middle and super-middleweight world champion and, despite his posturing style and contradictory manner, his overall record is impressive.

RIGHT: The dreadlocked Nigel Benn landing a punch on Vincenzo Nardiello on his way to winning the WBC super-middleweight title at the London Arena on 22 July 1995.

The cruiserweight class was instigated in 1979 by the WBC for fighters who couldn't compete with the heavyweights: Marvin Camel was the first winner, outpointing Yugoslavia's Mate Parlov in a second meeting. The WBA and IBF followed in recognising the class, the former terming it junior-heavyweight; though, in 1988, Evander Holyfield unified the cruiserweight titles, by relinquishing the belt to move up to heavyweight, he threw matters into confusion once more.

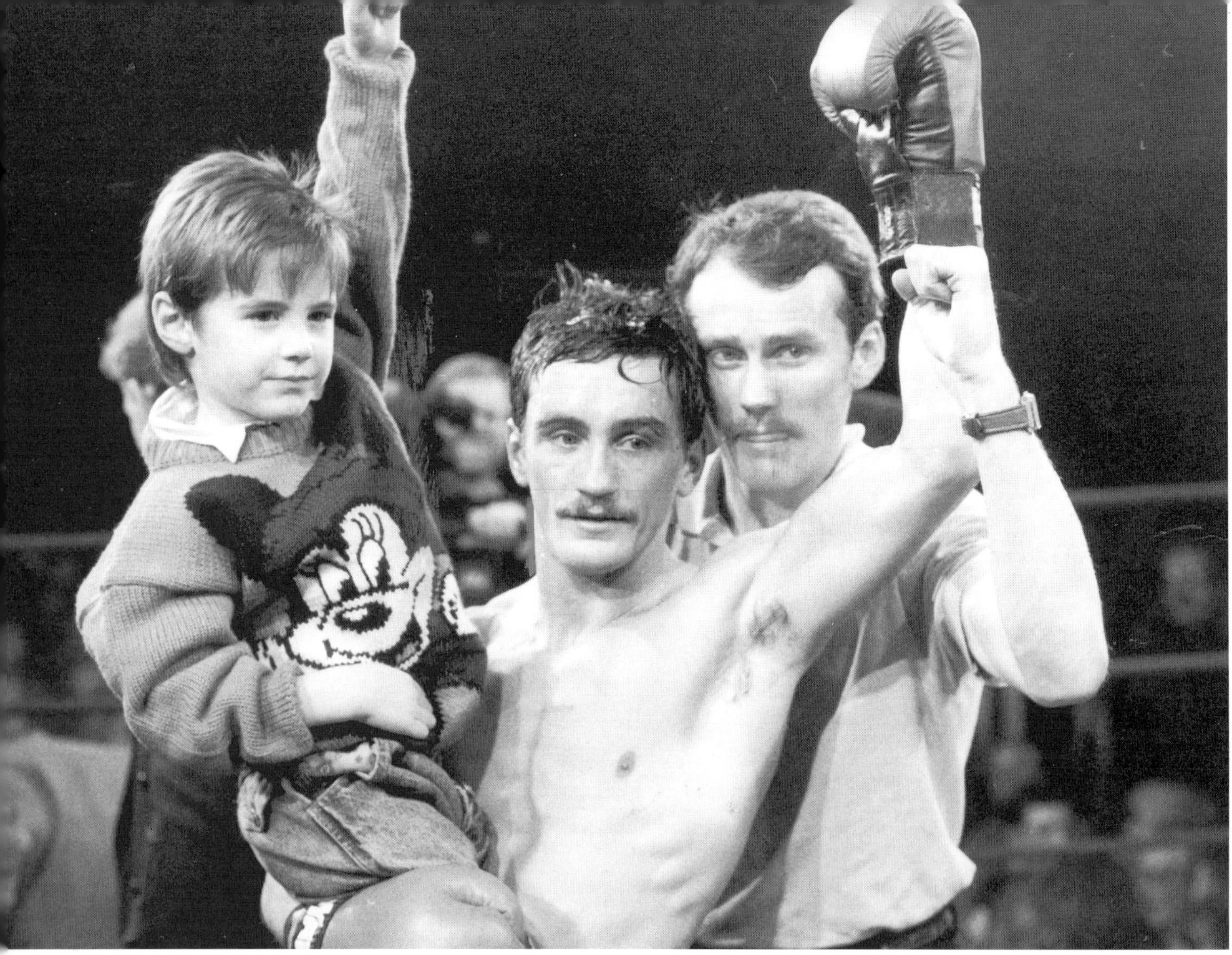

Scotland's Jim Watt had seemed a worthy successor to Ken Buchanan in the lightweight arena, defending the WBC lightweight crown four times after succeeding Roberto Duran in 1979, but his hopes bit the dust two years later when Alexis Arguello of Nicaragua, previously an outstanding super-featherweight, outpointed him to take the title. Watt would go on to become a respected ringside commentator.

The International Boxing Federation was formed in 1983 by a breakaway group from the WBA under would-be president Bobby Lee. The new body made its first mark on the sport in the following year when the super-middleweight class came into being. Designed to fill the yawning,

ABOVE: Barry McGuigan towards the end of his career in 1988. His was an unfulfilled talent and his record bears the closest inspection. Unfortunately he spent too much time outside the ring arguing with his manager, Barney Eastwood.

PREVIOUS PAGE: 8 December 1990 — just another day at the office for Mike Tyson as he puts out Alex Stewart in the first round of their heavyweight fight. It was Tyson's 39th victory.

stone-plus gap between light-heavy (175lb) and middleweight (160lb), it would yield some able champions following Scot Murray Sutherland's inaugural win. Indeed, boxers from the British Isles seemed particularly suited to the weight, supplying three further champions in Chris Eubank (WBO, 1991), Nigel Benn (WBC, 1992) and Steve Collins (WBO,

1995). Sugar Ray Leonard also briefly graced the class on his way up to light-heavyweight.

The year of 1983 saw Puerto Rican Wilfredo Gomez relinquish the world super-bantamweight title having established a record of 17 defences, all inside the distance, that had put him on the map. He'd move up to win two more WBC world crowns in the featherweight and junior-lightweight arenas before retiring at the end of the decade.

The WBA's featherweight title belonged to Ireland in 1985 when Barry McGuigan usurped Eusebio Pedroza, the Panamanian then making his 20th defence of a title first won in 1978. McGuigan took the title in London but was seen as a unifying influence back home, being a Catholic who'd married a Protestant and represented both halves of the divided island. His reign was short, losing to Steve Cruz in 1986 after perhaps rashly travelling to the strength-sapping heat of Las Vegas, and though his opponent would fail to hold onto the title McGuigan's was the greater fame. He remains well-known today for his TV punditry.

If boxing's heavyweight division is measured in eras, then 22 November 1986 will go down in history as raising the curtain on the Tyson era. It was then that 'Iron' Mike became the ever youngest heavyweight champion, taking the WBC title from Trevor Berbick at the age of 20 years and five months.

So complete was Tyson's domination of the top division that, by the time James 'Buster' Douglas caused perhaps the biggest shock in boxing history by knocking him out on 11 February 1990, he'd only been troubled by four punches in his life! One of those was thrown by British heavyweight hopeful Frank Bruno who landed a right hand in their first meeting in 1989. Then, as in 1996 when they met again in very different circumstances, Big Frank came off very much second best.

Mike Tyson putting Michael Spinks on the canvas in the first round of their world heavyweight championship fight in Atlantic City in June 1988.

ABOVE: Denis Andries fighting Australian Jeff Harding — the third of a trio of hard-fought encounters. Andries took on Harding for the final time in London in September 1991 and was beaten on points.

RIGHT: Anything but friendly — Riddick Bowe and Evander Holyfield in their rematch in Las Vegas, November 1995. Holyfield regained the crown Bowe had won in a great fight in 1993.

FOLLOWING PAGE: Riddick Bowe knocks down Herbie Hide for the fourth time in their fight in March 1995.

Douglas's feat proved very much a one-off: his Tokyo KO of Tyson was followed by a third-round demolition by Evander Holyfield and a swift return to obscurity. But if 'Iron Mike' had temporarily met his match in the east, he'd soon find an even less forgiving opponent in the law. An encounter not in the ring but an Indianapolis hotel room with one Desirée Washington led to accusations of rape and criminal deviate conduct. A guilty verdict resulted, but in the end Tyson served just over half of his six-year sentence and emerged in 1995 with a burning desire to regain his crown.

His return path to the top encompassed Peter McNeeley and Buster Mathis before Frank Bruno, who'd taken the WBC title by beating Oliver McCall, once again came into his orbit. It took Tyson just three rounds to repeat his 1989 victory and confirm he was once again the name to be feared. Unfortunately for him, he slipped up against the veteran Evander Holyfield in 1996 in what was the sport's biggest shock since Buster Douglas. There seemed little doubt, though, that 'Iron' Mike would come again.

Like the IBF several years before, the World Boxing Organisation came about in 1988 as a result of a breakaway group from the WBA, headed by Luis Salas. They were protesting at what they saw as violations of the WBA constitution, but the latest branch of the Alphabet Boys received scant support in some countries such as Japan and Britain which would not permit boxers to contest WBO titles.

British boxing was in the ascendant in

MGM GRAND GARDEN
Bank of America

7:56
RIDDICK BOWE
FILA

ABOVE: Chris Eubank went to Cork for the WBO super-middleweight championship rematch with Steve Collins in September 1995.The result was the same as that of their first match: Collins won on points.

the early part of the 1990s. In the light-heavyweight division, Dennis Andries made history by winning the WBC title for the third time when he knocked out challenger Jeff Harding in seven rounds, while two years later super-bantamweight hopeful Duke McKenzie beat classy American Jesse Benavides to become the first British boxer ever to claim world titles in three weight divisions. He'd try for a fourth in October 1994, moving up a division to take on featherweight holder Steve Robinson, but it proved a step too far. Nevertheless this product of a famous family had gone a long way.

RIGHT: Look at my belt, Harry! A jubilant Frank Bruno showing off his WBC belt after beating Oliver McCall at Wembley in September 1995.

Amazingly, as McKenzie's dreams ended, Andries, born in Guyana, would fight on through to 1995, when he was well beyond the age of 40 to take the British cruiserweight title. His longevity may be ascribed to the fact that he'd joined the management of Thomas

WORLD CHAMPION
WBC

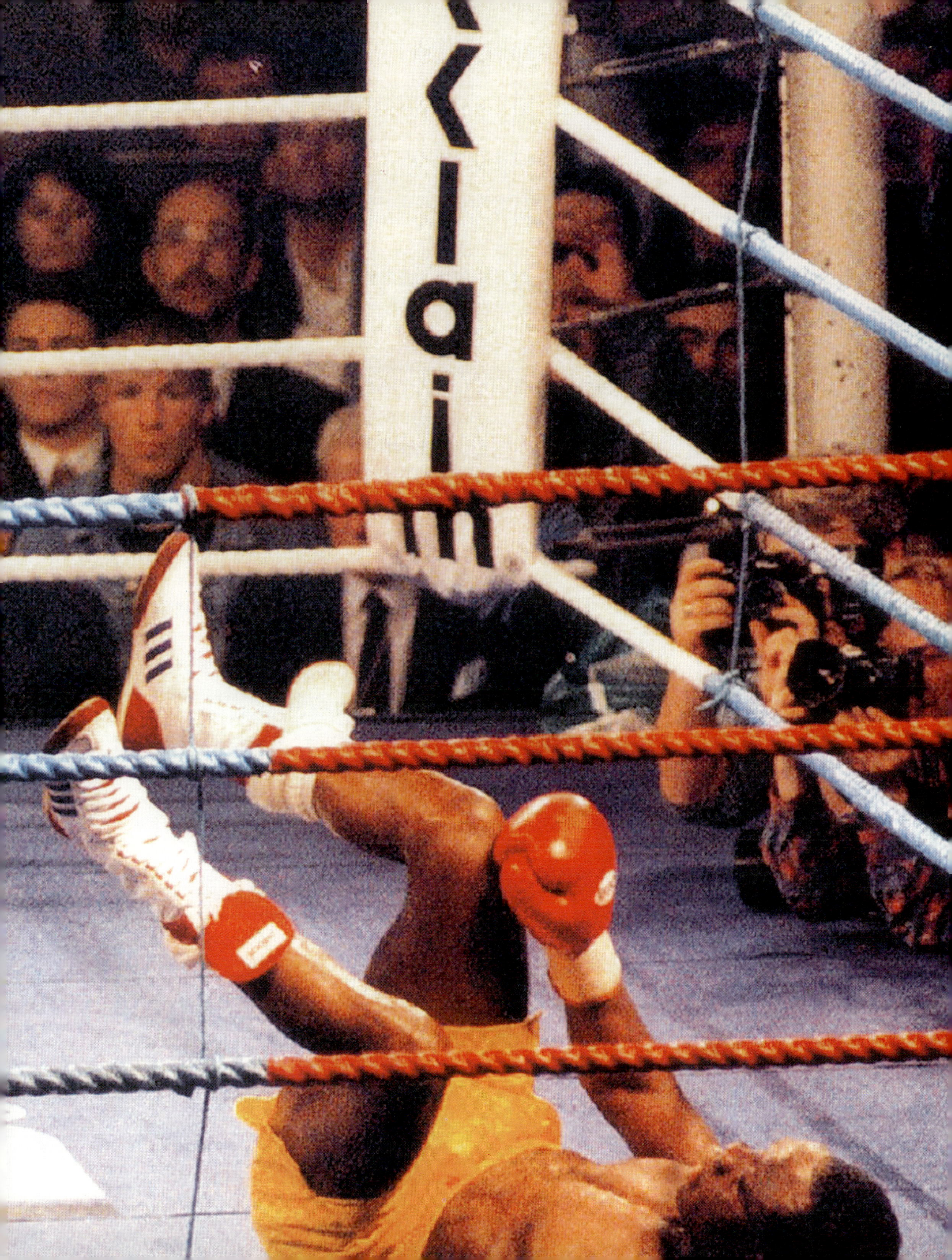

'Hitman' Hearns after losing to him in 1987.

The incurable disease AIDS had swept the world and it was no longer possible for boxing to ignore its deadly progress. The IBF was first in 1993 to stipulate testing for the HIV virus, the forerunner to full-blown AIDS, before each and every world title fight, and this was quickly adopted throughout boxing. Colombian Ruben Palacios was the first to fall at this

ABOVE: Prince Naseem Hamed standing in triumph over Juan Polo Perez as he knocks him over in the 2nd round at the Royal Albert Hall in July 1995.

RIGHT: Nigel Benn — the 'Dark Destroyer' — living up to his name as he lands a punch on Gerald McClellan in February 1995 during their WBC middleweight fight at the Docklands Arena.

McCLELI
FORREST
ALD

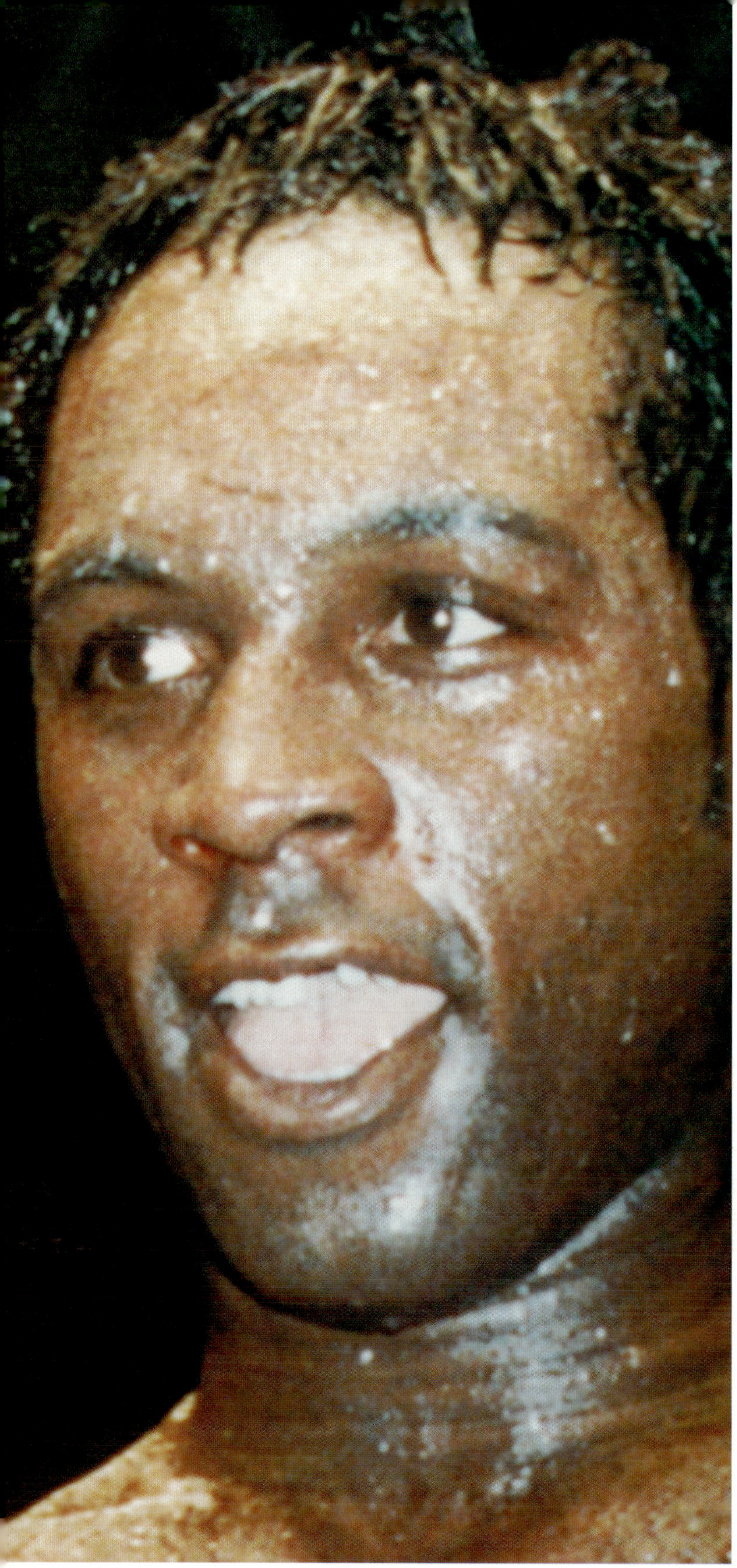

Born on 22 January 1964 in London, the 'Dark Destroyer' is one of the best English fighters ever — and certainly one of the bravest. Here he is seen celebrating after beating Lou Gent in June 1993.

hurdle when in 1993 he defended his title against John Davison. Since that sad piece of boxing history, Tommy Morrison has been the highest-profile casualty, and he made a point of lending his name to the education process against the disease after pulling out of a 1996 fight. It is to be hoped that the incidence of such cases will diminish as sportsmen realise they are not superhuman and that they need to take as many precautions as the next man.

Evander Holyfield, a 1984 Olympic champion, had been the lucky inheritor of the WBC/WBA/IBF heavyweight title without having to face Mike Tyson, having beaten the 'one-off' James 'Buster' Douglas in 1990. Having defended against three opponents, including George Foreman and Larry Holmes, he lost his title to Riddick Bowe but regained it on points in 1993 when their fight was famously interrupted by a man on a paraglider. Holyfield in his turn lost to Michael Moorer in 1994, and a knockout from Bowe the following year proved a crushing blow.

The Mexican Julio Cesar Chavez enjoyed a decade at the top of boxing, and put his country on the fight map. He was intent on registering an unbeaten century of fights, but the plot took an unfortunate turn when in 1994 he lost the WBC light-welterweight title to Frankie Randall. He avenged his first defeat in 91 fights by regaining the title, having previously been world champion at super-featherweight and lightweight, boxing on to justify critics' judgement that he was the greatest fighter of his era.

In the 6th round of their heavyweight title fight in Atlantic City in October 1995, Tommy Morrison is trying to catch his breath whilst down on one knee while Lennox Lewis stands menacingly over him.

Age rarely becomes an issue in boxing — but in November 1994 George Foreman became the oldest ever world champion at any weight when, aged 45 years and 10 months, he wrested the WBA and IBF heavyweight titles from the grasp of Michael Moorer. This was the culmination of a number of battles, the most notable having been fought in a Las Vegas court-room in August. 'Life, liberty and the pursuit of happiness are alive and well — and I'm living proof of it,' he smiled. And he was still smiling after landing a 10th-round knockout blow.

Britain had enjoyed a brief spell of heavyweight glory when Frank Bruno had won a world title at the fourth attempt, before Mike Tyson took less than three rounds to sink him in Las Vegas. In the middleweight division, they had seen a decade of success from Chris Eubank, who wrested the WBO crown from countryman Nigel Benn in 1990. He went on to become super-middleweight champion before losing twice to Dubliner Steve Collins in 1995.

There was, of course, always a danger inherent in boxing — a fact underlined by Eubank's fight for the WBO super-middleweight crown against Michael Watson in September 1991. Watson, many people's tip for the title, put up a plucky performance and was stopped in the 12th and final round, but was left wheelchair-bound through injuries sustained. It was something that clearly affected Eubank, as you would expect, and he never seemed the same fighter after. Another serious casualty was Gerald McClellan, who suffered permanent damage after his 1995 clash with Nigel Benn. Both these tragedies brought understandable headlines.

The rapid rise of Naseem Hamed, born in Sheffield of Yemeni parents, made him one of the brightest hopes of the British boxing firmament in the late 1990s. He became the jewel in promoter Frank Warren's stable, moving from bantam to featherweight in 1995 and storming unbeaten through the opposition. Though opinion was divided as to his merits beneath the hype, he could point to his record as proof that he backed up words with actions — and there was little doubt that in the wake of the well-meaning but limited Frank Bruno a world champion with staying power was exactly what Britain needed.

The continuation of boxing as an Olympic event was clearly crucial in bringing promising youngsters into the sport — and when Juan Antonio Samaranch, president of the International Olympic Committee, chose the 1992 games to state that 'Boxing will eventually lose its prison as an Olympic sport' all looked bleak. The Programme Committee of the IOC swung a further low blow when they recommended that the sport be dropped from 2000. Fortunately, this threat seemed likely to be a hollow one.

As the moral majority continued its crusade to stamp out boxing as a 'blood sport', the fight game seemed to survive — not only survive but in some areas thrive. Women's boxing has been one of the fastest-growing areas of the sport, and in 1994 history was made when an exhibition bout was, for the first time ever, include as a part of the US Boxing Championships.

Boxing has always aroused strong emotions both in its supporters and critics, but it seems certain that this compulsive sport will continue for the foreseeable future.

McCall knocks out Lennox Lewis in September 1994.

ATOMIC

ATLANTICO
ATLANTI
Nintendo

EVERLAST

ABOVE LEFT: Super lightweight champion Julio Chavez fighting Andy Holligan (right) in 1993; he won with a technical knock-out.

LEFT: The paucity of talent in the current boxing scene is perhaps best shown by the success of old stagers like Foreman and, illustrated here beating Rocky Pepeli, Larry Holmes.

THIS PAGE: Since 1994 Prince Naseem Hamed has been unbeatable; in 1997 he recorded his 26th straight win — against European featherweight champ Steve Hardy. Here he celebrates a 1995 victory.

FOLLOWING PAGE: Trevor Berbick feels the power of Mike Tyson in 1986. Tyson became the youngest heavyweight champion ever.

The Boxers

Muhammad Ali

NATIONALITY	WEIGHT(S) FOUGHT	NO. OF FIGHTS	WON–LOST (KO's)	HONOURS
American	Heavyweight	61	56-5 (37)	World heavyweight 1964-67, 1974-78, 1978-79

Clay stands over 'Sonny' Liston at the end of their second fight.

MOTORMOUTH Muhammad Ali not only became the most famous boxer of the late 20th century but also a bona fide celebrity, a man who could hold his own outside the boxing ring as spokesman for and figurehead of black culture round the world.

Born as Cassius Clay in Louisville, Kentucky on 17 January 1942, Ali took up boxing at the age of 12. He first came to prominence at the Olympic Games in Rome in 1960 when he won the light-heavyweight gold medal and returned to the States resolved to be a world-beater — which, as his subsequent record, 61 fights consisting of 56 wins (37 KOs), amply testifies, he became.

He set off after the heavyweight title in 1961, victories over such respected veterans as Sonny Banks and Archie Moore launching him to national prominence. With his lightning-fast blows and with his 'Ah'm the greatest' calling card, Ali totally revitalised the boxing scene in the early 1960s and became big box-office wherever he fought.

On 18 June 1963, Ali came to England for the legendary match against British heavyweight champ, Henry Cooper. Despite Cooper — in Ali's words 'a real professional' — flooring the American in the fourth, his opponent came back and, with his extraordinary combinations of punches, opened up Cooper's face to such an extent that the fight was stopped in the fifth. Even though he'd defeated the local hero, Ali was to become a much-loved figure in Britain in subsequent years.

He finally won the world heavyweight crown in 1964 in a grudge match with Sonny Liston. It was at this time that he became a Black Muslim, changed his name and began to fight not just for himself but for his people. He maintained his pole position — fending off bids from the likes of Floyd Patterson, Brian London and Ernie Terrell — until 1967 when his stand against US involvement in the Vietnam War and refusal to enlist into the army got him stripped of his title. He even had his passport taken away.

He was eventually reinstated and made a successful comeback in October 1970 against Jerry Quarry, whom he stopped in the fifth round. He subsequently despatched Oscar Bonvena and was ready to have a go at reigning champ Joe Frazier at Madison Square Garden on 8 March 1971. In a savage contest for which each man was paid $2,500,000, Frazier emerged triumphant — and when Ken Norton broke Ali's jaw in 1973 it looked like he was finished for good. But when the two met again six months later, Ali won on points and a re-match between him and Frazier was convened for 28 January 1974. By then Frazier had lost the world title to George Foreman, but Ali managed to beat his old rival on points and was ready to bid for the championship again.

Foreman and Ali fought it out in Kinshasa, Zaire, West Africa on 30 October 1974 and, against the odds, Ali beat the powerful Foreman, dodging his hammer-like blows and finally KO'ing his opponent with a right hook to Foreman's jaw in the seventh. He maintained his title until 1976 Olympic gold medallist, Leon Spinks surprisingly beat him on points. A re-match was duly convened on 15 September 1978 at the Superdrome in New Orleans — the largest indoor attendance in the history of boxing with a gate of $4,806,275 — where Ali taught the young reigning champion a lesson winning on points after a fairly unremarkable 15 rounds.

For a third time Ali was the world champ but he graciously retired at the end of 1978 — aside from a couple of sad comebacks in 1980 and 1981. Fighting off illness, Ali has subsequently worked to combat the poverty facing people in Third World countries, but will surely always be remembered as the greatest heavyweight of the 20th century.

Terry Allen

BORN Edward Govier in 1924 in North London, Terry Allen came from a tough background — his mother died when he was a baby and he'd been brought up by his blind grandmother. As a lad he was soon working as a barrow boy in Islington and fought more than a hundred bouts under his real name before turning professional in 1942.

He saw active wartime service as a navy stoker and was soon winning contests as part of the Mediterranean Fleet against a string of Egyptian flyweights, bantamweights and featherweights. He took on the name of Terry Allen when demobbed in deference to the memory of a close friend killed in action. He resumed his professional career, boasting a winning combination of determination and aggression. His first major tournament was against Ulsterman, John Joseph 'Rinty' Monaghan in April 1947, Allen only making flyweight status due to a recent bout of malaria. The little Cockney was KO'd in the first round — his first defeat in 40 fights.

Allen met 'Rinty' again two years later when the latter was world champion: though Allen had the Irishman down in the second round, the match was finally judged a draw. But Monaghan retired his crown, and it took the pugnacious Allen only two fights to win the flyweight title on points against Honore Pratesi on 25 April 1950. He arguably fought more 15-round contests than any other post-war English boxers with nine of the eleven in his career going the full distance.

Allen won both the European and the British titles during his career but was not destined to hold on to either for long.

NATIONALITY	WEIGHT(S) FOUGHT	NO. OF FIGHTS	WON–LOST (KO's)	HONOURS
British	Flyweight	77	62-14-1 (18)	European flyweight 1950 British flyweight 1951-52, 1952-54

Dennis Andries

NATIONALITY	WEIGHT(S) FOUGHT	NO. OF FIGHTS	WON–LOST (KO's)	HONOURS
Guyanian	Light Heavyweight	62	48-12-2	WBC Light-heavyweight 1986-1987 1989, 1990-1991 British Light-heavyweight 1984-86 WBC Continental Americas 1990 British cruiser-weight 1995

GUYANA-BORN Dennis Andries (born 5 November 1953) is living proof of what can be achieved through hard work and desire. His limited repertoire in the ring is borne out by an uninspired amateur career and an 11-year wait as a professional before winning a British title, outpointing Tom Collins to lift the light-heavyweight crown in 1984.

But from this inglorious beginning grew an improbable world champion. After winning a Lonsdale belt outright Andries — whose strength and durability were making him a man to be avoided — wrested the WBC light-heavyweight crown from American J. B. Williamson in London in 1986. However, it was a defeat, in his second defence against Thomas 'Hitman' Hearns, that was to shape a remarkable career.

Andries switched his base to the famous Kronk gymnasium in Detroit, where Hearns and many other world champions prepared for battle. Still ungainly but supremely fit and confident, Andries, claiming to be older than his official 36 years, regained the title in 1989 with a fifth-round stoppage of Tony Willis in Arizona. Then came a memorable three-fight series with Australian Jeff Harding, who stopped Andries in the last of 12 punishing rounds only to be knocked out a year later as the Briton became the first boxer from his adopted country to regain a world title twice.

After two successful defences, Andries took on Harding for the final time in London in September 1991 and was beaten on points. Undaunted by this defeat, Andries continued to box and in 1995, aged 42 (at least) won the British cruiserweight crown only to lose it later that year. A memorable character who fought with his heart as well as his fists, Andries was awarded an MBE in 1991.

Alexis Arguello

NICARAGUA would do well to produce another Alexis Arguello (born 19 April 1952), who rose from the back streets of Managua to become one of the best world champions of the 1970s and early 1980s. Indeed, his overall record of 22 world title fights (three defeats) marks him as one of the finest ever 'little men'.

NATIONALITY	WEIGHT(S) FOUGHT	NO. OF FIGHTS	WON–LOST (KO's)	HONOURS
Nicaraguan	Featherweight, Super-featherweight, Lightweight	88	80-8 (64)	WBA featherweight 1974-1977 WBC super-featherweight 1978-1980 WBC lightweight 1981-1982

Arguello, forced by poverty to ply his trade professionally at a mere 16, quickly impressing promoters and public alike with his fast hands and stylish combinations and he was nominated to take on WBA featherweight champion Ernesto Marcel in Panama City in early 1974, only to be outpointed over 15 rounds.

Success, however, was not a long time coming and Arguello was crowned king in November of the same year when he knocked out Marcel's conqueror, legendary former bantamweight champion Ruben Olivares, in 13 rounds. Four successful defences, all inside the distance, followed before weight problems saw Arguello move up to super-featherweight in 1978 and win the WBC title, which he successfully defended eight times, seven opponents failing to hear the final bell.

Not content with his achievements, Arguello went up to lightweight and came to Britain to end the reign of Scotland's WBC title holder Jim Watt over a fiercely contested 15 rounds in June 1981. After four further successes, Arguello attempted to win a fourth world title at light-welterweight but was stopped in 14 rounds by WBA champion Aaron Pryor after an unforgettable battle. Knocked out in the rematch a year later in 1983, Arguello retired to return in 1995, his money lost in the Nicaraguan Civil War. At his best, the handsome Latin will be remembered as one of boxing's finest stylists.

Henry Armstrong

NATIONALITY
American
WEIGHT(S) FOUGHT
Featherweight, Welterweight, Middleweight
NO. OF FIGHTS
174
WON–LOST (KO's)
145-9-20 (98)
HONOURS
WBC featherweight, lightweight and welterweight 1937-1940

HENRY Armstrong was born on 12 December 1912 in Columbus, Mississippi. His record of 145-20-9 (98 KOs), though obviously a remarkable one, does not tell the whole story about this amazing boxer.

After a stint as a successful amateur he turned professional aged 19, with his first pro bout in 1931. Known fondly in the business as 'Homicide Hank', he took the first of his world titles after defeating featherweight Peter Sarron and then quickly went on to secure the lightweight belt from Lou Ambers. Armstrong failed to make the featherweight limit ever again and Ambers took the lightweight crown back — but as a welterweight 'Hank' was invincible.

Armstrong made 19 consecutive title defences in just 28 months. Only heavyweights Joe Louis and Larry Holmes ever produced more. The frequency with which he accepted title fights was truly remarkable. In 1939 Henry Armstrong fought five championship bouts in the month of October, winning all five — four of them with knockouts.

Armstrong appeared in 26 world title fights, second only to Joe Louis' 27. His great strength was his speed and ability to attack: rarely did 'Hank' need to rely on defence. His feat of three simultaneous titles may never be broken and, incredibly, during that same period Armstrong was only denied a fourth world crown when he was held to a draw by middleweight Ceferino Garcia.

In later years, 'Homicide Hank' took on a more spiritual type of opponent after becoming the Reverend Armstrong — but he will always have a place among the all-time boxing greats.

Max Baer

BORN in Omaha Nebraska, on 11 February 1909, Nebraska, Max Baer was one of the hardest punchers the sport has ever known. More than that, an engaging personality made him one of the most popular outside the ring.

After moving to California, Baer began his boxing career in 1919, where his 6ft 2in, 200lb physique saw him knock out 20 of his first 28 opponents. However, after a lean spell, culminating in a lacklustre defeat by Paulino Uzcudun in 1931, most ring critics were ready to write him off. Two years later, Baer proved them wrong with a 10-round technical knockout of former champion Max Schmeling in New York.

That surprise victory earned him a tilt at the world crown, held by Primo Carnera, a year later at Long Island. Baer destroyed the huge Italian-American in 11 rounds — after knocking him down 11 times — to become world champion. But Baer's tenure was short, and within 12 months he was outpointed by James J. Braddock over 15 rounds.

Following a four-round KO by the up and coming 'Brown Bomber', Joe Louis, Baer briefly quit the ring, before returning to fight and beat such luminaries as Wales's Tommy Farr and the dangerous Tony Galento. But he finally hung up his gloves in 1941 after two losses to Lou Nova.

In all, Baer won 65 of 79 fights, 50 by knockout, and after turning his back on boxing made several films, including *The Harder They Fall.* His son, Max Baer Junior, became a household name in a hit television series of the 1960s *The Beverly Hillbillies.*

NATIONALITY	WEIGHT(S) FOUGHT	NO. OF FIGHTS	WON–LOST (KO's)	HONOURS
American	Heavyweight	79	65-14 (50)	World heavyweight champion 1934-1935

Wilfred Benitez

WILFRED Benitez ranks as one of the most stylish boxers of the modern era who, at the age of 17, became the youngest fighter in history to win a world title — the junior-welterweight crown.

Born on 12 September 1958 in the tough school of the Bronx, New York, Benitez was a precocious talent who turned professional at the tender age of 15. But Benitez had the misfortune to rise to prominence at the same time as two other great fighters — Sugar Ray Leonard and Tommy 'Hitman' Hearns.

After defending the junior-welterweight title three times, Benitez moved up a weight and beat welterweight holder Carlos Palomino to gain his second title in 1979. However, Leonard's stock was rising and the two came together for a classic encounter of speed and grace, in which Benitez was stopped in the 15th round.

The setback did not deter the brilliant New Yorker and he gained his third title in as many classes by knocking out Britain's WBC light-middleweight champ Maurice Hope in 1981, only the seventh fighter in history to achieve that feat.

After successful defences against tough opposition, Carlos Santos and the remarkable Roberto Duran at Caesar's Palace 12 months later, Benitez took on Hearns. After a dazzling 15 rounds, the Memphis-born, Detroit-based Hearns dethroned Benitez on a majority decision.

Benitez failed in a bid for middleweight honours, losing to Mustafa Hamsho, and his return to junior-middleweight was no more successful when he suffered a two-round KO by former champ Davey Moore. Benitez retired in 1990.

NATIONALITY	WEIGHT(S) FOUGHT	NO. OF FIGHTS	WON–LOST (KO's)	HONOURS
American	Light-welterweight, welterweight, middleweight	62	53-8-1 (31)	WBA light-welterweight 1976-1977 WBC welterweight 1979 WBC light-middleweight 1981-1982

Nigel Benn

NATIONALITY	WEIGHT(S) FOUGHT	NO. OF FIGHTS	WON–LOST (KO's)	HONOURS
British	Middleweight, super-middleweight	46	42-3-1	Commonwealth middleweight champion 1988-1989 WBO middleweight champion 1990 WBC super-middleweight champion 1992-1996

BORN on 22 January 1964 in London, the 'Dark Destroyer' is one of the best English fighters ever - and probably the bravest. The former soldier won the ABA middleweight title in 1986 and after turning professional won his first 21 contests, 11 of them in the first round.

The courage of Benn, and the fact that he never knew when he was beaten, would be more evident in his later bouts. Early on, his ability as a fighter - he could box comfortably with either hand, and could mix it with the best of them if required - proved too much for most of his opponents.

He went to the United States and stopped the much respected Doug DeWitt in his own backyard. If that didn't convince the Americans that Benn was a force to be reckoned with, his next win, inside a round over the formidable Iran Barkley, made the boxing world sit up and take notice.

Benn suffered the first setback of his career when he was knocked out in a bruising encounter with the then-immaculate Chris Eubank. The rematch ended in a controversial draw, most neutrals concluding the 'Dark Destroyer' had done more than enough to win. In-between those two contests Benn had beaten Mauro Galvano to secure the WBC super-middleweight championship. But Nigel Benn's greatest effort in a boxing ring was to end in tragedy.

On 25 February 1995, he took on the awesome Gerald McClellan. Benn was almost knocked out in the first, but somehow recovered to win with a 10th-round stoppage. Tragically, the fight had taken more out of his opponent than anyone at first realised and McClellan suffered brain damage. After losing his WBC crown to Thulane Malinga on a split decision Benn decided to call it a day. He was tempted back into the ring for two defeats against Steve Collins. Those last two contests are best forgotten and cannot detract from what was an outstanding career in the ring.

Michael Bentt

TRAGICALLY Michael Bentt enjoyed only a short career as a professional, but in a mere 13 bouts carved out a reputation as a formidable fighter.

Bentt was born in the South London suburb of East Dulwich in 1965 but his family moved to Jamaica — where he first picked up his basic boxing skills — when he was six and then on to New York when a teenager. He held both British and US citizenship, enabling him to carve out a highly successful amateur career on both sides of the Atlantic. He became the first to win the American national heavyweight title a total of five times, and was the New York Golden Gloves champ for four years. He also boxed for the British national team, but his amateur career ended when he failed in his bid to represent the US in the 1986 Olympics in Seoul when he was beaten by Ray Mercer in the trials.

Life as a pro got off to a rocky start when noted southpaw Jerry Jones KO'd him in the first round of his first contest. Then taken under the wing of manager Stan Hoffman who, along with former light-heavyweight supremo Eddie Mustafa Muhammad, worked wonders on his self-esteem and skill. He won 10 fights in a row and was then matched against WBO champ Tommy Morrison who wanted a warm-up prior to his crack at wresting the WBC heavyweight crown from Lennox Lewis.

The fight took place on 29 October 1993 in Tulsa, Oklahoma. It was to be an historic occasion, with a confident Morrison expecting few problems from his opponent. All looked rosy after he landed a mean left hook on Bentt's reputed 'glass jaw'. It looked like the favourite would finish it, but Bentt sized up the situation, capitalised on a moment of Morrison's carelessness and let fly with a supercharged right-hander that knocked him to the canvas. As he struggled to his feet, Bentt sent him tumbling twice and the fight was stopped after a mere 93 seconds!

Sadly his next fight in London against Herbie Hide ended in defeat in the seventh round. He subsequently collapsed in his dressing room, was rushed to hospital and was diagnosed as suffering from a brain disorder which curtailed a most promising career.

NATIONALITY	WEIGHT(S) FOUGHT	NO. OF FIGHTS	WON–LOST (KO's)	HONOURS
British/US	Heavyweight	Detailed stats not available	Detailed stats not available	American heavyweight champion WBO heavyweight champion 1993-94

TREVOR Berbick may well go down in history as the man who beat 'the greatest', Muhammad Ali, in his last big match in Nassau in the Bahamas on 11 December 1981. In reality, though, it was a far from exciting match with an overweight Ali losing on points to a solid and persistent opponent over 10 rounds.

Berbick won the WBC heavyweight title in Las Vegas on 22 March 1986 against Pinklon Thomas in 12 rounds, but was back there defending his crown later the same year against a young man of iron, Mike Tyson.

As with so many others since, the fight practically finished his career. In just two rounds Tyson mercilessly destroyed the reigning champ to become the youngest ever holder of the WBC heavyweight title — at a mere 20 years and 4 months!

Outside the ring Berbick's life also slumped. He turned to God, adopted an Afro name of Obim Tedechi but his financial dealings faltered and he was pressed by the authorities. Sadly, too, his other and final claim to fame was also a dubious one. In June 1988 he faced Carl Williams and made the record books by throwing the least punches — just four — in a round (the first)! Not surprisingly, Williams subsequently beat this 'blubberweight' on points over 12 rounds and Berbick was again a subject for the history books.

Trevor Berbick

NATIONALITY	WEIGHT(S) FOUGHT	NO. OF FIGHTS	WON–LOST (KO's)	HONOURS
American	Detailed stats not available	Detailed stats not available	Detailed stats not available	WBC heavy-weight champion 1986

Riddick Bowe

RIDDICK Bowe is one of boxing's great dilemmas. He looked the part, indeed at times he was the part, but too many times he failed to deliver. Born (on 10 August 1967) and raised in Brooklyn, his hero was Muhammad Ali — and while he may have been aiming high in trying to emulate him, for a while it looked as if he was on the right lines. In 1989, his first year as a pro, Bowe won all his 13 fights. Victories over Pinklon Thomas, Bert Cooper, Tyrell Biggs, Tony Tubbs and Pierre Coetzee set him up for a shot at Evander Holyfield for the undisputed heavyweight championship of the world in 1992. The critics called it one of the best fights the sport has ever seen, and it was Bowe who emerged the victor from this epic contest.

Bowe was then supposed to defend his title against Lennox Lewis — he refused — and the WBC stripped him of the title, following which he lost much of the credibility he had earned by fighting several no-hope opponents. By the time he entered the ring again to defend his WBA and IBF titles in a rematch with Evander Holyfield, rumours concerning Bowe's passion for junk food seemed to be correct as he looked more than a little overweight. In the end Bowe put on a game performance, but the fitter Holyfield deservedly won back his crown. Bowe may yet have a future in boxing, but it is looking more and more likely that he will be remembered as the man who failed to fulfil his potential.

NATIONALITY	WEIGHT(S) FOUGHT	NO. OF FIGHTS	WON–LOST (KO's)	HONOURS
American	Heavyweight	41	39-1-1	WBC,WBA and IBF heavyweight champion 1992 WBA and IBF heavy-weight champion 1993 WBO heavy-weight champion 1995

James J. Braddock

JAMES Joseph Braddock was born in New York on 7 June 1906 and must rank as one of the most unlikely heavyweight champions of all time.

A professional fighter from 1926, Braddock failed in a bid to lift the light-heavyweight crown in a 15-round bout against Tommy Loughran three years later. After that his career went into free-fall with 16 defeats in four years to the likes of John Henry Lewis and Al Gainer. But writer Damon Runyon did not give Braddock the nickname the 'Cinderella Man' for nothing, and his boxing renaissance was truly remarkable.

Living on public assistance and seemingly at the end of his career, Braddock beat Lewis in a rematch — and, after clinching a points victory over Art Lasky, took on power-punching Max Baer for the world title.

The popular Baer was a 10–1 favourite, but Braddock, having suffered in the Depression, took his opportunity and produced the fight of his life and with slick boxing outpointed Baer over 15 rounds to record one of the greatest upsets in the history of the sport.

But Braddock's time in the spotlight was to be brief. In 1937, he took on the great Joe Louis and, in spite of putting down the young 'Brown Bomber' in the first, Braddock valiantly relinquished his crown to his Alabama-born opponent after eight brutal rounds.

Braddock's last hurrah was a points decision over Tonypandy's ambitious young turk Tommy Farr. He then retired with 51 victories from 85 bouts, 26 coming by way of knockouts.

NATIONALITY	WEIGHT(S) FOUGHT	NO. OF FIGHTS	WON–LOST (KO'S)	HONOURS
American	Heavyweight	86	46-23 -17	World heavyweight champion 1935-1937

Frank Bruno

NATIONALITY	WEIGHT(S) FOUGHT	NO. OF FIGHTS	WON–LOST (KO's)	HONOURS
British	Heavyweight	45	40-5 (38)	WBC heavyweight champion 1995-1996 European heavyweight champion 1985

THE former WBC heavyweight champion was born in London on 16 November 1961. His fight record of 41-5 (38 KOs) was an impressive one, though at times the British boxer was criticised for taking on a number of opponents with 'hollow chins'.

Bruno's first professional bout was in 1982 — an easy first-round win over Lupe Guerra. He then enjoyed a number of comfortable victories over a succession of little-known boxers. A setback for Bruno in 1984 saw him lose in 10 rounds to James 'Bonecrusher' Smith.

Big Frank then began his quest for a world title with wins over opponents including Larry Frazier and Gerrie Coetzee. That set up a WBA heavyweight clash with Tim Witherspoon at Wembley Stadium and, though Frank put up a gutsy effort, the American took the fight in the 11th.

Wins over James Tillis, Chuck Gardner, Reggie Gross and Joe Bugner set him up for at attempt to lift the undisputed heavyweight belt. Bruno put up the fight of his life before losing out in the fifth to Iron Mike Tyson.

Bruno fought for the WBC belt against Lennox Lewis and lost, but once again the 'True Brit' put all thoughts of quitting behind him and his determination was rewarded in 1995 when he won a points decision over Oliver McCall to secure the WBC heavyweight crown.

His joy was short-lived, however, as his first defence saw him lose in three to Tyson. It was a punishing loss and this time he decided to call it a day. Frank Bruno was a credit to the sport, but his inability to take a punch ultimately cost him dearly.

Joe Bugner

A BOXER blessed with the ultimate physique, Joe Bugner, born in Hungary on 16 March 1950 but raised in England, will be recalled primarily as the man who ended the career of British legend Henry Cooper.

Bugner, a huge man with a copybook technique, was judged by referee Harry Gibbs to have won Cooper's European, British and Commonwealth titles just days after his 21st birthday in 1971, a decision which turned the public against him. Bugner was soon to be relieved of his titles by Jack Bodell.

However, the European crown was back in his possession the following year and he went on to gain perhaps the biggest scalp of his career in former world champion Jimmy Ellis of America. But it was in defeat, against legendary heavyweights Muhammad Ali and Joe Frazier, that Bugner enjoyed his finest hours. Indeed, many thought he had earned the decision against the latter, after climbing off the floor to take the former world champion 15 rounds at Earl's Court. But given a shot at Ali's world title in Kuala Lumpur in 1975, Bugner hardly threw a glove in anger over 15 uninspiring rounds.

Following a brief retirement Bugner, goaded by British champion Richard Dunn, returned to answer his tormentor in one swift round but, disgruntled by the public's lack of affection, retired again — this time to Australia. A failed business venture saw him return 10 years later in 1987, when he was thrashed in eight rounds by Frank Bruno. Another comeback attempt in the 1990s was quickly curtailed by Scott Welch, and Bugner finally waved goodbye to the ring still dubbed the nearly man who should have delivered more.

NATIONALITY	WEIGHT(S) FOUGHT	NO. OF FIGHTS	WON–LOST (KO's)	HONOURS
British	Heavyweight	74	61-12-1	British heavyweight 1971 Commonwealth heavy-weight 1971 European heavyweight 1971, 1972-76

Tommy Burns

BORN Noah Brusso in Ontario, Canada, on 17 June 1881, Tommy Burns is ranked as one of the most unsung heavyweight champions ever.

Burns took his nom de guerre from a famous jockey of that time so that his parents, who frowned on his pugilistic ambitions, would not realise he was fighting. Burns, at 5ft 7in, is the shortest man ever to hold the title, but he was a superb boxer aided by an unusually long 74in reach.

The Canadian began fighting in 1900 and claimed the crown with a points decision after 20 rounds over Martin Hart, who had become champion following the retirement of James J. Jeffries. Burns was four inches shorter than Hart, but his superior boxing and punching power earned him a deserved victory.

After beating Fireman Jim Flynn and Jack O'Brien, Burns became the first heavy to defend his title outside the United States. He beat Jack Palmer and Gunner Moir in London before further successes in Dublin and Paris.

But time was running out for Burns and he was later accused of trying to dodge the great Jack Johnson, who eventually caught up with him in Sydney in 1908. The first black heavyweight champion annihilated his opponent in 14 rounds and treated Burns with such indifference that at one point he offered his chin for Burns to hit. He duly obliged, but with a morale-sapping lack of success.

Burns, in all, had 60 bouts, claiming 45 scalps, 35 by knockout and holds the record — with Larry Holmes — of eight straight KOs in 11 title defences. In 1948, the puncher turned preacher and was ordained in California.

NATIONALITY	WEIGHT(S) FOUGHT	NO. OF FIGHTS	WON–LOST (KO's)	HONOURS
Canadian	Heavyweight	60	45-6-9 (35)	World heavyweight champion 1906-1908

Hector Camacho

HECTOR 'Macho' Camacho has been a colourful character throughout his career. Born on 24 May 1962, the flamboyant Puerto Rican southpaw fighter has been in the news more than once for reasons other than boxing. But you don't go from being WBC junior-lightweight champion to IBC middleweight champion of the world without talent. Camacho certainly has that, notably in the speed of his hands and his ability to be an elusive man in the ring.

Some of his earlier career wins came against the likes of Cornelius Boza Edwards, Greg Coverson and Edwin Rosario. In 1983 he stopped Bazooka Limon in the fifth round to win the vacant WBC junior-lightweight belt. Camacho then had two 12-round battles with Greg Haugen, losing the first but winning the rematch, before stepping into the ring with Julio Cesar Chavez. Camacho took the legendary Mexican the distance but Chavez emerged the victor.

But the 'Macho Man' recovered, and in 1996 won a 12-round unanimous decision over Roberto Duran to capture the IBC middleweight championship. Hector Camacho recently thwarted another comeback of Sugar Ray Leonard and, though the years are starting to catch up with him, he shows no signs as yet of hanging up the gloves.

NATIONALITY	WEIGHT(S) FOUGHT	NO. OF FIGHTS	WON–LOST (KO's)	HONOURS
Puerto Rican	Super-featherweight, lightweight, light-welterweight	61	58-3	WBC super-featherweight champion 1983 WBC lightweight champion 1985 WBO light-welterweight champion 1989-91, 1991-1992

Tony Canzoneri

TONY Canzoneri boasted a 15-year career, became the sport's third three-division champion and still retains the record for the quickest knockout in a lightweight contest.

Canzoneri (born in Louisiana on 6 November 1908) turned professional in 1925 at the age of 16 and, two years later, fought out a draw for the vacant bantamweight title with Bud Taylor, only to lose the rematch a few months later.

However, he was undeterred by the setback and a few months later became world featherweight champion by beating Johnny Dundee on points. But Canzoneri lost the title to Andre Routis, before claiming the lightweight title in a lightning-fast 66 seconds first-round defeat of Al Singer.

Canzoneri then took on England's Jackie 'Kid' Berg in two epic fights, for the junior-welterweight crown, knocking his opponent out in three rounds. He retained his belt in the return with Berg, and was described as the best pound-for-pound boxer in the world.

Canzoneri held on to his lightweight crown but lost his junior-welterweight title to Johnny Jadick and then the lightweight to Barney Ross. After losing to Ross in Chicago, who was booed by his hometown fans after the decision, Canzoneri failed to recapture it later in 1933.

But two years later he was champion again, regaining the title from Lou Ambers on points over 15 rounds. But, like many others before and since, Canzoneri outstayed his welcome inside the ropes and retired after being knocked out in three rounds by welterweight Bummy Davis in 1939. But he bowed out boasting a record of 139-24-10 with 44 KOs.

NATIONALITY	WEIGHT(S) FOUGHT	NO. OF FIGHTS	WON–LOST (KO's)	HONOURS
American	Featherweight, lightweight, light-welter-weight	173	139-24-10 (44)	World feather-weight champion 1928, World light-weight champion 1930-1933 World light-welterweight champion 1931-32, 1933

Primo Carnera

PRIMO Carnera was born in Italy on 26 October 1906, and after starting his pro career in Paris in 1928, moved to the United States two years later.

At 260lb and over 6ft 5in tall, Carnera was the heaviest of all world champions, but most observers felt his victories in Europe were pre-arranged and did not treat his aspirations or ability with too much seriousness.

However, the Italian-American proved his critics wrong when, in 1933, he knocked out Jack Sharkey in six rounds in New York. The friendly giant was immediately afforded celebrity status and used his engaging personality to good advantage outside of the ring.

But his hold on the heavyweight belt was brief and one year later, again in New York, he was clubbed to defeat in 11 rounds by the hard-punching and flamboyant Max Baer. After two successive knockouts by Leroy Haynes, he returned to Europe practically penniless, having seen little of the purse money he had won in the States.

From 1928 to 1945 Carnera had 99 bouts, winning 86 — 66 by knockout. In the Second World War, he was a member of the Italian Sniper Brigade, had a losing fight and returned to the ring in the US, this time as a wrestler.

Fortunately for the likeable, but gullible Carnera, this proved more successful and he was able to retire after winning a small fortune. He appeared in several films, most notably *On The Waterfront*, playing a hoodlum alongside stars Marlon Brando and Rod Steiger.

NATIONALITY	WEIGHT(S) FOUGHT	NO. OF FIGHTS	WON–LOST (KO'S)	HONOURS
Italian	Heavyweight	103	88-14-1	World heavyweight champion 1933-1934

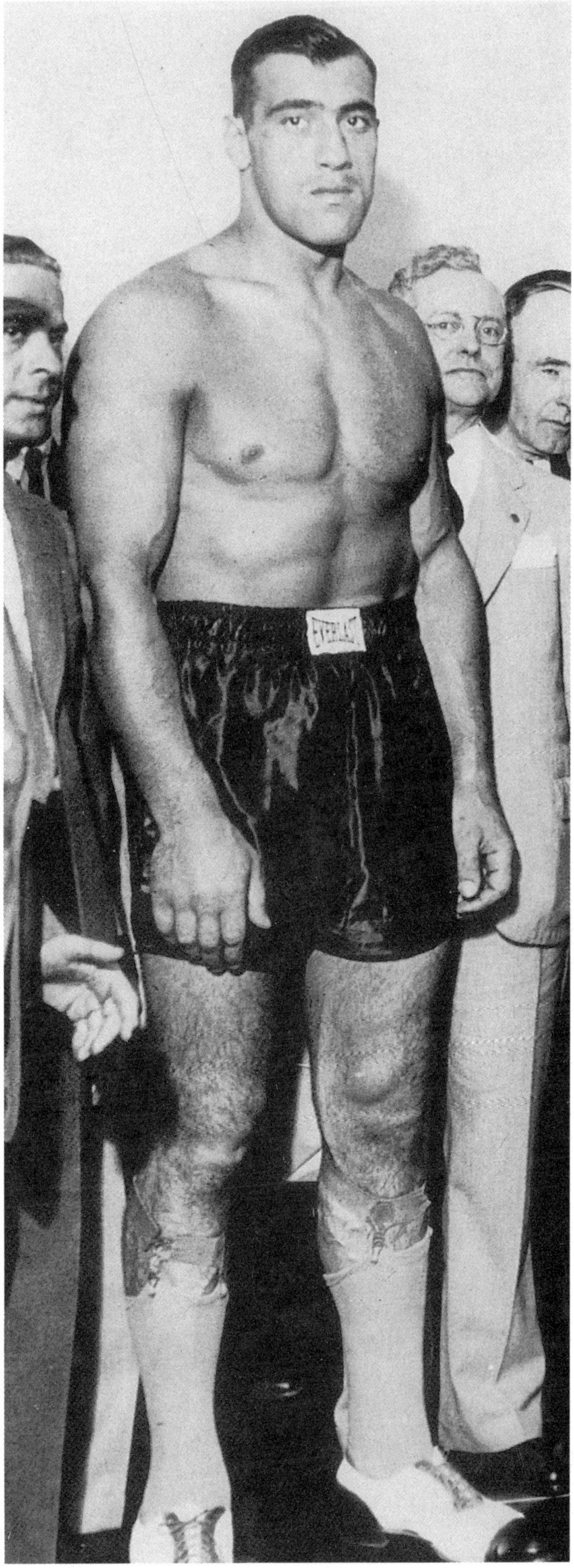

Ezzard Charles

EZZARD Charles was born in Georgia on 7 July 1921 but raised in Cincinnati and, although he became world heavyweight champion, most observers felt he would have been better as a light-heavyweight.

After an unbeaten amateur career, Charles turned pro in 1940 and quickly earned the nick-name of the 'Cincinnati Cobra', for the quickness and potency of his attacks. He started out as a middleweight, scoring a decision over future champion Joey Maxim. However, service in World War II kept Charles inactive, but once hostilities had ceased he returned to the ring with a vengeance.

He beat the great Archie Moore in 1946 and squared contests with Jimmy Bilvins and Lloyd Marshall at light-heavyweight before a tragic fight with Sam Baroudi — who died after the contest — made him alter his style.

But in 1948 Charles beat Jersey Joe Walcott for the vacant heavyweight championship and secured his reputation as a worthy champion with a points decision over the ageing Joe Louis. Charles defended his title once more against Walcott and Maxim, who was the world light-heavyweight champion, before succumbing to Walcott in a third world title contest.

The emergence of the awesome Rocky Marciano signalled the end of Walcott's reign and, in 1954, Charles was once again involved in a heavyweight battle. Marciano's advisers saw Charles as an easy defence, but were proved wrong and the 'Rock' pronounced his 15-round points decision the hardest of his career. Charles hung up his gloves four years later with a record of 96-25-1.

NATIONALITY	WEIGHT(S) FOUGHT	NO. OF FIGHTS	WON–LOST (KO's)	HONOURS
American	Heavyweight	122	96-25-1 (58)	World heavyweight 1948-54

Dave Charnley

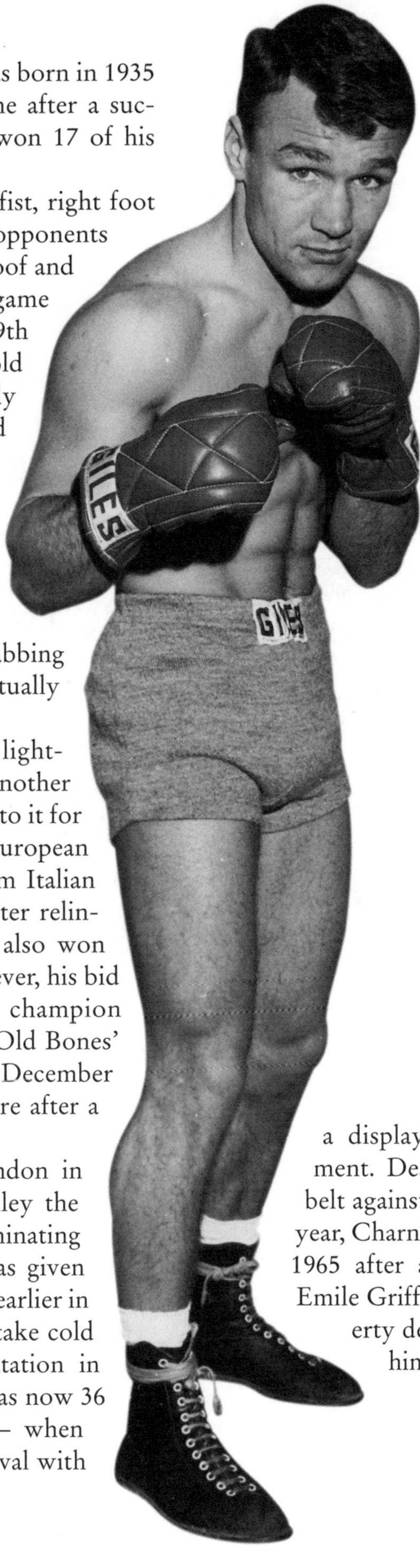

NATIONALITY
British
WEIGHT(S) FOUGHT
Lightweight
NO. OF FIGHTS
61
WON–LOST (KO's)
48-12-1 (30)
HONOURS
British lightweight 1957-63 Empire lightweight 1958-62 European lightweight 1960-63

SOUTHPAW Dave Charnley was born in 1935 and, after entering the fight game after a successful teenage amateur career, won 17 of his first 18 contests.

His ruthlessly efficient, right fist, right foot forward style saw him despatch opponents with ease and he cultivated an aloof and dispassionate attitude to the game rare in his contemporaries. His 19th pro fight was against 24-year old Sammy McCarthy, who'd recently lost the British flyweight title and had subsequently gone up a notch in the divisions. The 'hard man' floored McCarthy for nine in the second round and eight in the third and, despite a comeback in the fourth, Charnley's murderous rain of jabbing rights and hammer-like lefts eventually won him the night.

Charnley won the British lightweight crown in 1957 against another southpaw, Joe Lucy, and held on to it for six years. In 1960 he became European champ, winning the honour from Italian Mario Vecchiato — he would later relinquish that too, undefeated. He also won the Empire championship. However, his bid to make world lightweight champion foundered against reigning Joe 'Old Bones' Brown in Houston, Texas, in December 1959 when he was forced to retire after a clash of heads in the fifth.

A rematch, this time in London in 1961 also failed to bring Charnley the victory he craved: despite dominating the second half, 'Old Bones' was given the victory for skilful handwork earlier in the match. The Brit could only take cold comfort in their third confrontation in Manchester in 1963 — Brown was now 36 and no longer world master — when Charnley finally KO'd his old rival with a display of fierce body punishment. Despite winning a Lonsdale belt against Maurice Cullen the same year, Charnley retired from the ring in 1965 after a defeat by welterweight Emile Griffith to expand on his property dealings which would make him a millionaire.

Julio Cesar Chavez

JULIO Cesar Chavez can truly claim to be one of the all-time greats. The Mexican has been world champion at three different weights and has knocked out over 80 of his opponents. In return, he has been on the canvas just once in his career.

Born on 12 July 1962, Chavez turned pro in 1980 at the age of 17 and won 43 bouts before he beat Mario Martinez to claim the WBC super-featherweight crown in 1984. Three years later he took the WBA lightweight tile from Edwin Rosario before unifying two-thirds of the lightweight division with victory over Jose Luis Ramirez.

That, however, was a somewhat unsatisfactory win as the fight was stopped following an accidental head-butt to his opponent. Chavez was ahead on points and was awarded the contest. The tough little Mexican then defeated Roger Mayweather to take the WBC super-lightweight title. Possibly his most famous victory was when stopping IBF champion Meldrick Taylor with only two seconds of the fight remaining.

Chavez's bid for a fourth title failed when he was held to a draw by the WBC welterweight champion Pernell Whitaker. He lost for the first time against Frankie Randall, but won the rematch. It is a testament to Chavez that, despite the vast number of fights he has been involved with, his face remains virtually unmarked.

NATIONALITY	WEIGHT(S) FOUGHT	NO. OF FIGHTS	WON–LOST (KO'S)	HONOURS
Mexican	Super-featherweight, lightweight, light-welterweight	100	97-2-1 (79)	WBC super-featherweight champion 1984-1987 WBA lightweight 1987-1989 WBC lightweight champion 1988-1989 WBC light-welterweight champion 1989-1994, 1995- IBF light-welterweight champion 1990-1991

Steve Collins

IRISHMAN Steve Collins will always be remembered as the man who demolished boxing's 'Mr Cool', Chris Eubank, in a somewhat controversial match on 18 March 1995.

Collins, born on 21 July 1964 in Dublin, had embarked on his professional career by relocating to Boston, MA, as a 21-year old and had cultivated a strong reputation for himself — his first big claim to fame was taking WBA world middleweight holder, Mike McCallum the full 12 rounds in 1990 and only losing on points. In 1992, after McCallum had given up the title, Collins took on American Reggie Johnson and only lost on a split decision.

Returning to his native Ireland, Collins's career hit a slump, but his motivation returned when he resoundingly beat Chris Pyatt in 1994 in five rounds to win the WBO middleweight crown. He was the first world middleweight champion to come from Dublin.

In 1995 he faced his toughest challenge by stepping up a division to do battle with WBO super-middleweight supremo Chris Eubank. Collins spent the six weeks prior to the contest rigorously training in Las Vegas and had undergone hypnosis — which some say acted as a psychological weapon against Eubank, when the Irishman announced his use of this therapy just two hours prior to the fight.

While Eubank indulged in his usual razamataz entry into the ring, Collins quietly sat in his corner, mentally calm before the contest. It was a curious but close match with Eubank landing quality blows but Collins consistently on the offensive. The Irishman nearly KO'd the Londoner in the seventh with a brutal right-handed shot, but the bull-like Eubank came back and floored Collins with a right hook in the tenth. Collins was hurt, but hungry for the title — he got up and carried on, winning the match after 12 rounds, on a split decision.

Eubank, facing his first major defeat, made much of the hypnosis angle but when the pair met again in Cork four months later, Collins put on a show of such skill and fury that he completely outpointed his opponent and Eubank decided to retire! As well as calling time on Nigel the 'Dark Destroyer' Benn's career, there was clearly more to come from the devastating Dubliner.

NATIONALITY	WEIGHT(S) FOUGHT	NO. OF FIGHTS	WON–LOST (KO's)	HONOURS
Irish	Middleweight, super-middleweight	33	30-3	WBO middleweight champion 1994-1995 WBO super-middleweight champion 1995-

John Conteh

NATIONALITY	WEIGHT(S) FOUGHT	NO. OF FIGHTS	WON–LOST (KO's)	HONOURS
British	Heavyweight	39	34 -4-1	European light-heavy-weight champion 1973-1974 British and Commonwealth champion 1973-1974 WBC world champion 1974-1977

ARGUABLY one of the best all-round fighters Britain has ever produced, John Conteh (born on 27 May 1951) was a headline-writer's delight but his playboy image was probably to blame for his failure to produce the results his talents demanded.

A handsome Liverpudlian, Conteh was an outstanding amateur, winning ABA titles at middleweight and light-heavy and the Commonwealth Games middleweight gold medal in 1970, aged just 19. In his 19th fight as a professional, Conteh was light-heavyweight champion of Europe after beating Germany's Rudiger Schmidtke, and one bout later in 1973 he took Chris Finnegan's British and Commonwealth belts, successfully defending them in a bitter rematch.

Conteh, a superb all-round fighter and fierce competitor, was then pitched against Jorge Ahumada the following year for the vacant WBC crown and his arm was lifted in triumph after 15 bruising rounds. The world seemed there for the taking for the Toxteth boy with the film-star looks but, after three successful defences, his career was interrupted by a series of hand injuries and managerial bust-ups. Stripped of his title, Conteh attempted to regain it in 1978 against Mate Parlov in Belgrade but was the victim of an outrageously partisan points decision.

Two defeats by Matthew Saad Muhammad, the first a close points decision and the second a fourth-round stoppage, brought Conteh's career to an end, but the man wiped out in the second fight in Atlantic City in March 1980 bore no relation to the brilliant technician who had looked set to rule the division six years earlier.

Henry Cooper

NO boxer, past or present, can command a place in the hearts of the British fighting public like Henry William Cooper, born in Bellingham, London, on 3 May 1934.

Cooper, an artful boxer with a bout-winning left hook, turned professional in 1954 after twice winning the ABA light-heavyweight title. 'Our 'Enery' became Britain's longest-serving heavyweight champion (1959-71), won three European titles and three outright Lonsdale belts — all this after losing his first three title fights, twice to old rival Joe Erskine for the British championship and to Sweden's Ingemar Johansson for the European crown. But world glory was to elude him.

Like many British fighters, Cooper's career is brought to mind first and foremost by his defeats. In 1963, an up-and-coming young American heavyweight named Cassius Clay arrived in London for a non-title fight and was dumped on the seat of his pants for the first time ever, caught by Cooper's famed left hook. (See photograph at right.) Given time to recover by the infamous 'split glove' incident during rounds, Clay — later to become Muhammad Ali — got off his stool to halt his rival on cuts, always Cooper's Achilles heel. Ali returned in 1966 to offer Cooper a shot at his world title and stopped him — again on cuts — in six rounds.

Cooper's last fight, against a young Joe Bugner in 1971, was probably his most controversial. Defending his British, European and Commonwealth crowns, Cooper was on the wrong end of a points decision and promptly retired on a wave of public emotion. An OBE, Cooper's popularity on the showbiz circuit remains intact to this day.

NATIONALITY	WEIGHT(S) FOUGHT	NO. OF FIGHTS	WON–LOST (KO'S)	HONOURS
British	Heavyweight	55	40-14-1	British and Empire (later common-wealth) heavyweight champion 1959-69, 1970-1971 European champion 1964, 1968-69, 1970-71

James J. Corbett

THE name of James John Corbett is synonymous with finesse and led to what came to be called scientific boxing or the Queensberry Rules.

Born in California on 1 September 1866, 'Gentleman Jim' — as he was and still is widely known — came to prominence by knocking out Joe Chomsky over 27 gruelling rounds. Two years later in 1891, Corbett, giving away over a stone in weight, went 61 rounds with the highly-rated Peter Jackson before the bout was declared a non-contest affair.

One year later, as a 4-1 underdog, Corbett fought the brutish John L. Sullivan for the world title — a case of brains versus brawn. Sullivan had not fought for over three years and the more stylish Corbett outboxed him throughout before executing the coup de grace in the 21st round to become world champion.

Corbett successfully defended his title against Charley Mitchell in three rounds and, in the first fight to be filmed as a motion picture, KO'd Peter Courtney in an exhibition bout.

But, in 1897, he met Cornishman Bob Fitzsimmons in Carson City and was knocked out in the 14th round. He twice fought again for the world title against James J. Jeffries — Fitzsimmons' successor — before hanging up his gloves in 1903.

He fought just 19 times, winning seven by knockout, four by decision, had two draws and lost once on a foul. After retiring, Corbett took leading roles in several plays, including George Bernard Shaw's *Cashel Byron's Profession*, and was considered by many a more than competent actor.

NATIONALITY	WEIGHT(S) FOUGHT	NO. OF FIGHTS	WON–LOST (KO's)	HONOURS
American	Heavyweight	19	11-4 -4	World heavyweight champion 1892-97

Don Curry

NATIONALITY	WEIGHT(S) FOUGHT	NO. OF FIGHTS	WON–LOST (KO's)	HONOURS
American	Welterweight	400	397-3	WBA welterweight champion 1983-86

DON 'Cobra' Curry (born 7 September 1961) was hailed by most boxing critics as the best pound-for-pound fighter in the world at his peak in the early 1980s and, but for weight problems, must surely have gone on to be one of the all-time greats.

Curry was a prolific amateur, winning all but three of over 400 fights, and the welterweight gold medal at the Moscow Olympics in 1980 would have been his for the taking but for the American boycott. However, he was to take handsome recompense as a pro, quickly becoming a title contender before outpointing Korean Junsok Hwang for the WBA belt in his home town of Fort Worth, Texas, in 1983. Brilliant defensive skills, combined with lethal two-fisted attacks, stamped him the complete fighter.

Curry, extremely tall for a welterweight at over 5ft 10in, ran up a sequence of impressive defences, including a second-round knockout of top challenger Milton McCrory in 1985. But, despite serving several notices he would move up a weight, he took one fight too many at 10st 7lb, looking well below strength as Britain's Lloyd Honeyghan handed him a shock first defeat in Atlantic City in late 1986.

This proved a pivotal fight in Curry's career. Up to light-middleweight, he was spectacularly knocked out by Mike McCallum the following year and, though he won Gianfranco Rosi's title in Italy in 1988, his air of invincibility had gone forever.

He lost his WBC crown to Frenchman René Jacquot before failing gallantly against IBF middleweight champion Michael Nunn in Paris in 1990.

Oscar De La Hoya

BORN on 4 February 1973 in Montebello, California, Oscar De La Hoya is well on his way to establishing himself as one of the all-time greats. His first bout in 1992 saw him win within one round and he quickly established himself as a fighter with a clinical finish — pounding his next 20 opponents into defeat with only John John Molina and Mike Grable able to go the distance. Then, in what was billed as the biggest lightweight unification fight in 10 years, De La Hoya destroyed IBF champion Rafael Ruelas with an awesome display of punching inside two rounds.

The next challenge saw Oscar display his incredible courage as he fought and overcame the then-undefeated Genaro Hernandez. Fighting without his left arm for most of the fight because of injury, De La Hoya was powerful and brave enough to win inside six. His biggest test to date came in 1996 when he took on the legendary Julio Cesar Chavez for the WBC super-lightweight championship. The tough, experienced Mexican was no match for De La Hoya and the fight was halted in the fourth.

For all his power inside the ring Oscar De La Hoya is a contented, humble man outside of his work. Nearly always wearing a smile, his face is seen on numerous product endorsements, proving that his popularity stretches to well beyond sport. Touted as the noble art's next sensation, the man as yet shows no sign of failing to deliver on that score.

NATIONALITY	WEIGHT(S) FOUGHT	NO. OF FIGHTS	WON–LOST (KO's)	HONOURS
American	Lightweight	22	22 (20)	WBO super-featherweight champion 1994 WBO light-weight champion 1994-95 IBF light-weight champion 1995 WBC light-welterweight champion 1996-97 WBC welter-weight champion 1997-

WILLIAM Harrison Dempsey, nicknamed the 'Manassa Mauler' after his birthplace in Colorado (on 24 June 1895), is regarded by many as the apotheosis of professional fighters.

Dempsey left home at 16 and learned his trade in the school of hard knocks on the road living as a hobo, before he started boxing under the ring name of 'Kid Blackie'. After compiling a number of impressive knockout victories, Dempsey challenged Jess Willard for the world title in 1919.

The 37-year old champion proved to be no match for the young, hungry Dempsey and was despatched in three rounds in Toledo after being floored seven times in the opening round.

Even more primitive in its intensity was his first defence against Argentine challenger Luis Angel Firpo in New York. Firpo, too, was downed seven times after the first bell but, unbelievably, knocked Dempsey through the ropes and out of the ring. Dempsey recovered, with the aid of a few willing hands, and went on to stop Firpo in the next round.

Dempsey's fame had softened him and, after three years of inactivity, he met the smooth ex-Marine Gene Tunney and lost his title in a clear 10-round decision. But Dempsey, ever the fighter, returned a year later in 1927 to beat future champion Jack Sharkey and set up a return with Tunney.

Dempsey forfeited his chance of a seventh-round knockout by failing to go to a neutral corner and Tunney recovered to win another 10-round decision. Dempsey, who figured in the first $1 million fight with Georges Carpentier, retired immediately after, boasting a record of 62-6-10, 51 wins by knockout.

NATIONALITY	WEIGHT(S) FOUGHT	NO. OF FIGHTS	WON–LOST (KO's)	HONOURS
American	Heavyweight	78	62-6-10	World heavyweight champion 1919-26

Jack Dempsey

James 'Buster' Douglas

THE former heavyweight champion of the world won 30 of his 37 fights but will always be remembered for just one of them. The 6ft 4in boxer turned pro in 1981 but led an undistinguished career until he recorded wins against ranked contenders Randall Cobb and Greg Page. When the IBF stripped champion Michael Spinks of his belt it set 'Buster' up for a world title tilt against Tony Tucker. But Douglas put up an uninspired performance and Tucker took the title. Douglas then won a another series of fights against little-known boxers, the only exception being former WBC champion Trevor Berbick.

So when James Douglas (born 7 April 1960 in Ohio) entered the ring to face Mike Tyson in Tokyo on 10 February 1990 there were few — including Douglas himself — who expected an upset. His odds of 44-1 against were said to be the longest ever offered in a world title clash. But Douglas went out and put on the show of his life. After causing Tyson all sorts of problems throughout the contest, the challenger caught him with solid punches in the 10th and 'Iron' Mike was knocked out.

Douglas later admitted that he didn't really enjoy his time as WBC champion of the world — and certainly by the time he took to the ring again to defend the belt against Evander Holyfield it was painfully obvious that his training had more than fallen by the wayside. Holyfield won the fight with some considerable ease against an overweight opponent.

So James 'Buster' Douglas may well just be remembered for that one fight against Mike Tyson — but then so he should be. It was one of the upsets of all time. You can't take that away from the man.

NATIONALITY
American
WEIGHT(S) FOUGHT
Heavyweight
NO. OF FIGHTS
36
WON–LOST (KO's)
30-5-1
HONOURS
WBC, WBA and IBF heavyweight champion 1990

Terry Downes

A former US Marine, Paddington-born Terry Downes (born 9 May 1936) overcame his boxing inadequacies — a tendency to cut, a questionable defence and the lack of a real knockout punch — with a sheer, indomitable spirit and will to win which helped him achieve his goal to become a champion of the world.

Back in his native England in 1957 after a spell Stateside with his family, Downes turned pro and was British middleweight champion within two years. Following an impressive eliminator victory over the cagey Joey Giardello, Downes challenged Paul Pender for his world title in 1961. But the American, who had beaten the legendary Sugar Ray Robinson the previous year, stopped Downes in the seventh round after opening a severe cut across the British scrapper's nose.

Downes, though, was to have his moment of glory six months later. On 11 July 1961, Pender — ahead on points in a return bout in London — failed to answer the bell for the 10th round in controversial circumstances, claiming exhaustion. In their third and final meeting the following April, Pender regained the title on points.

Downes fought on and beat his boyhood idol Robinson, way past his prime, in late 1962. But he almost went out with a bang two years later when, fighting at light-heavyweight, he was close to stealing Willie Pastrano's world title before being stopped in the 11th. Downes, seen by the working-class British public as one of their own, went on to fill his coffers as a successful bookmaker.

NATIONALITY	WEIGHT(S) FOUGHT	NO. OF FIGHTS	WON–LOST (KO'S)	HONOURS
British	Middleweight	44	35-9	British middleweight champion 1958-59, 1959-62 New York and European recognition as world middleweight champion 1961-62

Roberto Duran

NATIONALITY	WEIGHT(S) FOUGHT	NO. OF FIGHTS	WON–LOST (KO's)	HONOURS
Panamanian	Lightweight, welterweight, light-middleweight, middleweight, super-middleweight	111	99-12 (69)	WBA lightweight champion 1972-79 WBC lightweight champion 1978-79 WBC welterweight champion 1980 WBA light-middleweight champion 1983-84 WBC middleweight champion 1989-90

ROBERTO Duran is considered by many to be one of the best pound-for-pound fighters in the history of the game.

Duran (born 16 June 1951), who became known as 'Hands of Stone', grew up in Chorillo, Panama — as tough a playground as you can get for someone destined to hold world titles at four different weights. In one of the many anecdotes of the young Duran, he is reputed to have knocked down a horse with a single blow.

Duran quit school at 14, turned pro a year later and, in his first bout, beat soon-to-be junior featherweight champion Carlos Mendoza. But his rough edges needed honing and, under the supervision of New York trainers Freddy Brown and Ray Arcel, he beat Scotland's superb lightweight champion Ken Buchanan to become world title holder.

After 12 successful defences, the Panamanian challenged welterweight king Sugar Ray Leonard and, in the 'Brawl in Montreal', Duran captured the title on points over 15 vicious but brilliant rounds.

He had won all of his 14 title fights, with 12 coming by way of knockout, and — despite two losses in returns with Leonard — was the undoubted supreme boxer. His record stood at 73 victories, with just one loss against Esteban DeJesus, and 55 knockouts.

Three years after the first Leonard contest in 1980, Duran captured his third world title by knocking out Davey Moore to lift the WBA junior-middleweight championship. Six years later, he was at it again — this time beating Iran Barkley to gain the middleweight crown.

Chris Eubank

LOVE him or loathe him, Chris Eubank (born 8 August 1966) kept British boxing in the news during his reign as middle and super-middleweight world champion and, despite his posturing style and contradictory manner, his overall record is impressive.

London-born Eubank moved to New York in 1985 where he turned professional, winning five fights before returning to England in 1987. Snapped up by new young promoter Barry Hearn, Eubank was pitched against fellow Briton Nigel Benn, the ferocious-punching WBO middleweight champion, three years later. After a fierce battle Eubank, who had absorbed his opponent's best punches and answered with some of his own, floored Benn in the ninth round to take his title.

After two somewhat uninspiring defences, Eubank took on the ill-fated Michael Watson and was awarded a dubious decision over 12 rounds. Three months later, having both stepped up to super-middleweight, the pair met again for the vacant WBO crown and the skilful Watson, ahead on points, was stopped in tragic circumstances in the last round, his brain injuries leaving permanent disabilities.

Naturally affected by this, Eubank fought a series of tepid matches until a second meeting with old adversary Nigel Benn, where he gained a controversial draw. But in 1995, after 15 successful defences, Eubank was finally outpointed by Irishman Steve Collins, who beat him again in a rematch. Despite his well-documented hatred of the sport, Eubank, monocle, cane and all, came out of retirement in 1996 as a self-promoted light-heavyweight and once more hit the world title trail.

NATIONALITY	WEIGHT(S) FOUGHT	NO. OF FIGHTS	WON–LOST (KO's)	HONOURS
British	Middleweight, super-middleweight	47	43-2-2	WBC international middleweight champion 1990 WBO middleweight champion 1990-91 WBO super-middleweight champion 1991-95

Chris Finnegan

NATIONALITY	WEIGHT(S) FOUGHT	NO. OF FIGHTS	WON–LOST (KO's)	HONOURS
British	Flyweight	77	62-14-1 (18)	European flyweight 1950 British flyweight 1951-52, 1952-54

Evans ducks under a Finnegan left, 1972.

DESPITE being forced to retire at the age at 32 because of a detached retina in his right eye, Chris Finnegan will always be remembered as one of the most fearless British boxers.

Chris had always learned how to take blows — he once admitted that his toughest beating was from an older brother! His experiences on various building sites also helped build the muscles necessary to take him up the ladder to become ABA light-heavyweight champion in 1966, beating Alexei Kiselyev in the final.

However, the title wasn't enough to win him a place in the British Commonwealth Games squad and it seemed he'd also miss the Olympics. But Chris went to Mexico and, despite some minor misdemeanours including a hilarious off-the-cuff remark to HRH Prince Philip, the so-called 'brawler' was the only British pugilist to return with a gold medal.

A noted southpaw, Finnegan was then groomed for professional life by Sam Burns and Freddie Hill, who broadened his range, and for his 15th fight was pitted against European middleweight champ Tom Bogs in August 1970. A similar close draw with German light-heavyweight Conny Velensek — whom he beat convincingly in a rematch — persuaded him to take on US heavyweight Bob Foster. Foster had defended his title many times and only lost to the best, Muhammad Ali and Joe Frazier; Finnegan showed amazing guts, persevering till the 14th when a left hook KO'd him.

Finnegan enjoyed success into the early 1970s, holding both the British and Commonwealth light-heavyweight crowns, and maintained a healthy rivalry with the younger John Conteh who'd recently won the European title. However both his bouts with Euro champ in 1973 and 1974 ended in defeat, Finnegan having to withdraw from both with a heavily bleeding head. He was still aiming for the top when partial blindness forced him to quit, but 'Fighting Finnegan' will always have a place in the hearts of the British public.

Bob Fitzsimmons

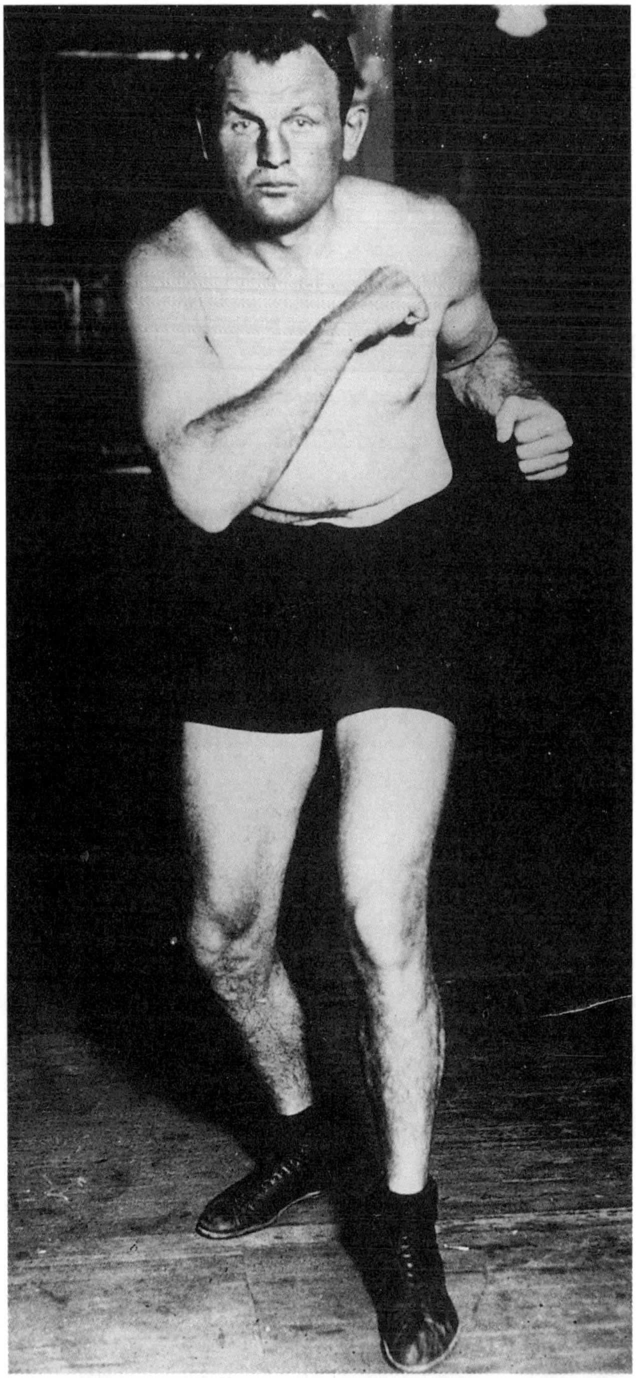

NATIONALITY	WEIGHT(S) FOUGHT	NO. OF FIGHTS	WON–LOST (KO's)	HONOURS
British	Middleweight, heavyweight, light-heavy-weight	62	40-11-1	World middleweight champion 1891-94 World heavyweight champion 1897-99 Light-heavy-weight champion 1903 -05

RUBY Robert Fitzsimmons, who was born on 26 May 1863 in Helston, Cornwall, but emigrated to New Zealand as a child, was one of the least likely-looking of world champions.

But Fitzsimmons, speckled with freckles and balding, deceived most of his opponents and was a title holder at three different weights. His upper-body strength, gained from his years as an apprentice blacksmith, served him well in his early years as a professional in Sydney, Australia, before settling in the United States.

Fitzsimmons' first world title came at middleweight when he stopped 'Nonpareil' Jack Dempsey in 13 rounds in New Orleans, but he defended the title only once — dismissing Dan Creedon in two rounds before moving up to heavyweight.

It was at this weight that Fitzsimmons first displayed his ferocious body punching, flattening Peter Maher in two contests. James J. Corbett defended his world title against the rugged Cornishman in 1897 in Carson City and took the early rounds where his superior jab peppered and bloodied his opponent's face. But Fitzsimmons kept pressing away and in the 14th round landed his renowned 'solar-plexus' punch to knock Corbett out and, at 167lb, become the lightest heavyweight champion in history.

He lost his title two years later to James J. Jeffries in an 11-round KO at Coney Island. Fitzsimmons, however, dropped down to light-heavy and defeated George Gardner in San Francisco over 20 rounds to win his final championship.

In 1914, three years before his death at the age of 54, Fitzsimmons retired, boasting a record of 40 wins — 32 by KO — and 11 defeats.

George Foreman

BORN on 22 January 1948 in Texas, Foreman is one of the most amazing men to ever grace the ring. After winning the gold medal at the 1968 Olympics he turned pro and proceeded to beat any opponent placed in front of him — most with considerable ease.

In 1973 Foreman, very much the underdog, challenged heavyweight champion Joe Frazier. After Frazier had been on the canvas six times the referee stopped the contest. But Foreman met his match the following year — though he did so against Muhammad Ali at his best. Soon after, he quit boxing to take up the role of ordained minister.

He remained in retirement for a decade before returning to the ring as the 'Punching Preacher'. Foreman then won 24 consecutive fights before losing on points to champion Evander Holyfield in 1992. Two years later, aged 45, he knocked-out IBF champion Michael Moorer to become the oldest man ever to win the heavyweight title.

He was deservedly named 1994 Fighter of the Year and even now, as a 48-year old, the 'Punching Preacher' may still have not finally retired.

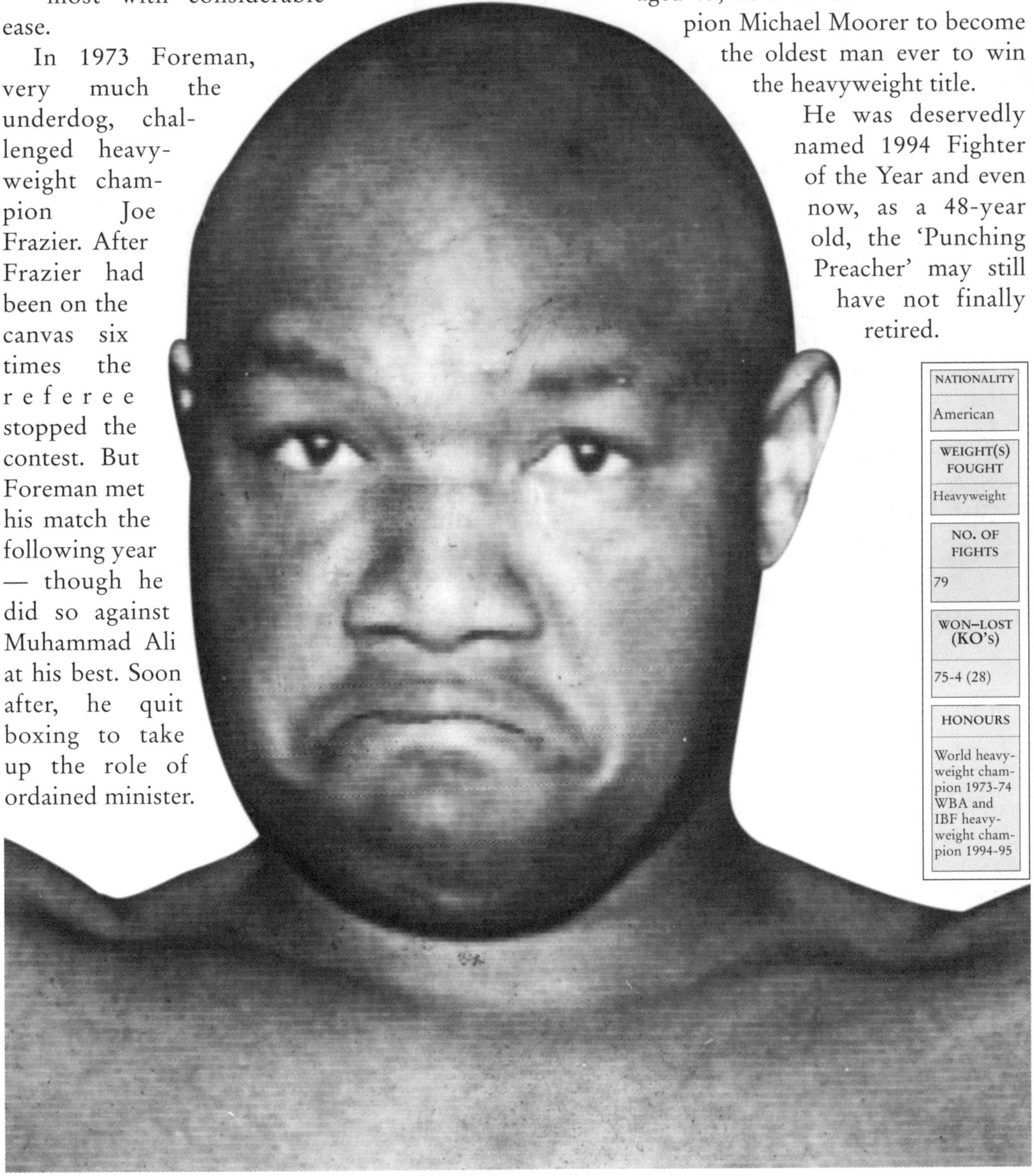

NATIONALITY
American
WEIGHT(S) FOUGHT
Heavyweight
NO. OF FIGHTS
79
WON–LOST (KO's)
75-4 (28)
HONOURS
World heavyweight champion 1973-74 WBA and IBF heavyweight champion 1994-95

Joe Frazier

'SMOKIN' Joe Frazier (born in South Carolina on 12 January 1944) was champion of the world at a time when the sport was brimming with top-class heavyweights, his reputation as a slugging, all-action fighter built on three epic battles with Muhammad Ali.

Beaten just twice as an amateur, both times by Buster Mathis, Frazier replaced his injured conqueror at the Tokyo Olympics in 1964 and returned with the gold. A pro the following year, Frazier quickly battered his way to the forefront of the rankings and, after Ali had been stripped of the world title for refusing to be drafted into the US Army, he met old foe Mathis for the New York version of the championship and halted him in the 11th. Two years later, in 1970, he unified the titles by handing WBA champion Jimmy Ellis a terrible beating in four one-sided rounds.

On 8 March 1971, the fight the world wanted to see took place in New York, when Frazier floored and outpointed the returning Ali over 15 rounds. However, jubilation turned to humiliation two years later when he was clubbed to defeat inside two rounds by the fearsome George Foreman.

A rematch with Ali in 1974 ended in a points defeat, but their final meeting a year later for Ali's world title in the 'Thriller in Manilla' went down in history as one of the finest fights ever, both men punching themselves to a standstill before Frazier remained seated after 14 rounds. 'Smokin' Joe fought on without success, but his rivalry with Ali and their mutual respect is written in boxing legend.

NATIONALITY	WEIGHT(S) FOUGHT	NO. OF FIGHTS	WON–LOST (KO's)	HONOURS
American	Heavyweight	37	32 -4-1 (27)	New York recognition as heavyweight champion 1968-70 World heavyweight champion 1970-73

Wilfredo Gomez

PINT-SIZED Puerto Rican Wilfredo Gomez (born 29 October 1956) was one of the most prolific and deadly punchers in the history of the sport. He held a world amateur title before turning professional in 1974 and during the early part of his career won 32 consecutive fights by way of knockout.

He won the first of his world titles in his 17th pro bout and, in doing so, displayed the formidable courage and resilience that would add two more. Gomez was forced to recover from a knockdown before dismissing super-bantamweight holder Dong-Kyung Yum in 12 rounds. He made a divisional record 17 successful defences before dropping the title in 1983.

Despite losing his first shot at the featherweight title with an eighth-round knockout against Salvador Sanchez, Gomez outpointed LaPorte for the WBC version in 1984 before Azumah Nelson KO'd him in 11 rounds a year later.

After losing to the immensely dangerous Nelson, the durable Gomez moved up a weight to controversially wrest Rocky Lockridge's junior-lightweight crown away from him on Gomez's home turf.

But, once again, Gomez's reign was a brief one, and he was knocked out in his first defence of the title by Alfredo Layne in nine rounds. This setback proved one too many for the great Puerto Rican, who immediately announced his retirement.

Gomez returned to the ring just one more time, in 1989, knocking out junior-welterweight Mario Salazar in two rounds before quitting for good with a record of 42-3-1 (40 knockouts).

NATIONALITY	WEIGHT(S) FOUGHT	NO. OF FIGHTS	WON–LOST (KO's)	HONOURS
Puerto Rican	Bantamweight, featherweight, junior-lightweight	46	42-3-1 (40)	WBC super-bantamweight champion 1977-83 WBC featherweight champion 1984 WBA junior-lightweight champion 1985-86

Marvin Hagler

NATIONALITY	WEIGHT(S) FOUGHT	NO. OF FIGHTS	WON–LOST (KO's)	HONOURS
American	Middleweight	67	62-3-2 (52)	Undisputed world middleweight champion 1980-87 WBC and IBF middleweight champion 1987

SOBRIQUETS in boxing are easily come by, but the tag 'Marvelous' Marvin Hagler (born 23 May 1952) barely does justice to one of boxing's fiercest fighting machines.

Newark-born Hagler was something of a slow starter, beaten twice early in his career (both subsequently avenged) and having to wait six years for his first world middleweight title shot after turning pro in 1973. Even this ended in failure, when he could only manage a draw against the pedestrian Italian Vito Antuofermo in Las Vegas in 1979. Then Antuofermo lost his crown to British southpaw Alan Minter and the rest, as they say, is history.

Hagler, shaven-headed and menacing, went to Britain in September 1980 and ripped away Minter's title, cutting his rival to shreds in three rounds. Bombarded by missiles from an unhappy crowd, Hagler vowed never to return to a British ring — a promise he was to keep — but took with him a new-found resolve which helped him dominate the middleweight division totally for the next six years.

Equally at home orthodox or southpaw, Hagler's clubbing two-handed attacks proved impossible to quell as he retained his title 11 times against the best his weight had to offer, including Willie Lee in one round, Roberto Duran on points and a memorable three-round demolition of six-time world champion Thomas Hearns.

His career ended in controversy with a disputed defeat against fellow-great Sugar Ray Leonard, Hagler retiring in disgust after a split-decision went against him. But 'Marvelous' Marvin unquestionably ranks as one of boxing's superstars.

Prince Naseem Hamed

SELF-STYLED 'Prince' Naseem Hamed is one of the great success stories of British boxing in the late 1990s. Born in Sheffield on 12 February 1974 of Yemeni parents and discovered as a seven-year old by trainer Brendan Ingle, Naseem won the National Schoolboy title five times and junior ABA title twice, and turned pro in 1992 without senior level experience.

His extrovert antics have done nothing to diminish his very real talents: in May 1994, he fought European bantamweight champ Vincenzo Belcastro in only his 12th bout and wrested the title from the veteran by winning each and every round. His strengths — speed of hand and foot, awkward style and above all confidence — were clear.

After one successful defence of the title, Hamed was forced to step up a division, but immediately took the WBC international super-bantamweight crown, beating Freddy Cruz in the sixth in front of his Sheffield home crowd. Moving up yet again to featherweight after five defences in a year, Naseem set his sights on unseating Welshman Steve Robinson who'd successfully defended the WBO world title seven times!

The two met at the Cardiff Rugby Club on 30 September 1995, and Robinson felt he had little to worry about in front of a rabid home crowd. However, a four-punch combination from the Prince in the fifth had the champ on the floor. After two more rounds of taking Hamed's supercharged punching, Robinson was losing ground and Naseem finished it in the eighth with a typically individual left hook right in Robinson's face.

His undefeated run continued through 1996 as he added the IBF featherweight crown to his collection with a win against highly-rated American Tom Johnson. Hamed laid both titles on the line in May 1997 against Billy Hardy knowing that win or lose he would still be the most talked-about man in the British fight game: he won in the first round.

NATIONALITY	WEIGHT(S) FOUGHT	NO. OF FIGHTS	WON–LOST (KO's)	HONOURS
British	Bantamweight, super-bantamweight, featherweight	20	20-0	European bantamweight champion 1994 WBC international super-bantamweight champion 1994-95 WBO featherweight champion 1995- IBF featherweight champion 1997-

Thomas Hearns

NATIONALITY	WEIGHT(S) FOUGHT	NO. OF FIGHTS	WON–LOST (KO's)	HONOURS
American	Welterweight, light-middleweight, light-heavyweight, middleweight, super-middleweight, light-heavyweight	61	56-4-1 (44)	WBA welterweight champion 1980-81 WBC light-middleweight champion 1982-86 WBC light-heavyweight champion 1987 WBC middleweight champion 1987-88 WBO super-middleweight champion 1988-91 WBA light-heavyweight champion 1991-92

THE most famous product of Manny Steward's legendary Kronk gymnasium in downtown Detroit, Thomas 'Hitman' Hearns boasts an astonishing career which has brought him world titles at six different weights from welter to cruiserweight.

Born in Memphis, Tennessee on 18 October 1958, Hearns at 6ft 1in was a freakish welterweight whose towering presence, 78in reach and awesome punching power quickly paved the way to the WBA version of the title in 1980. After three successful defences inside the distance he met the great Sugar Ray Leonard in a unification bout in 1981. Ahead on points and only needing to stay on his feet, Hearns could not contain a furious 14th-round onslaught from his desperate rival and was sent crashing to the canvas before the referee stepped in to rescue him.

Up at light-middleweight, Hearns took Wilfred Benitez's WBC title in 1982 before blitzing the much-feared Panamanian Roberto Duran in two rounds. After losing a short, sharp three-round war with middleweight champion Marvin Hagler in 1985 — the savage first three minutes, both fighters throwing every punch in their armoury, described as the best in boxing history — Hearns dethroned durable WBC light-heavyweight champion Dennis Andries two years later.

Hearns also collected versions of the middleweight (1987) and super-middleweight (1988) championships before, astonishingly, he completed a title six-timer at cruiserweight in the 1990s. At the time of writing, the 'hitman', an evergreen 38, was preparing for the 62nd fight of his illustrious career.

Herbie Hide

THOUGH born in Nigeria on 27 August 1971, Herbie Hide came to the UK as a two-year old and was brought up by a family in Norwich. As such he's regarded as one of the few recent great British hopes of heavyweight boxing alongside Frank Bruno and Lennox Lewis.

Known as the 'Dancing Destroyer', he reached the final of the ABA heavyweight competition aged 17, only to lose to Henry Akinwande, and turned professional a year later, winning all of his first 21 fights.

All the major titles fell into his lap: he was WBC international heavyweight champion 1992-94 and Penta Continental champ 1993-94. In 1993, having toppled overweight Michael Murray in the fifth, he became British heavyweight champ, a crown he never defended.

In 1994 Hide faced Michael Bentt for the WBO heavyweight title — it was a contest between two British giants and the match was scheduled for the New Den, Millwall FC's brand new football stadium, on 19 March 1994. It was prefaced by an ugly incident between the pair at a West End press conference, where Bentt allegedly goaded Hide and the two ended exchanging punches. The British Boxing Board of Control fined each fighter for their behaviour but the match went ahead as planned.

Bentt, who'd recently despatched Tommy Morrison in a first-round KO, was odds-on to win despite fitness problems, but after the rumble at the press launch Hide was determined to have his revenge. With his superior speed, Herbie handled Bentt with consummate ease and constantly landed blows on the face of his taller opponent. Bentt was flagging and by the seventh Herbie finished off with a clean KO.

Hide lost his first defence of the title in Las Vegas in April 1995, with the superior Riddick Bowe beating him in five rounds. He retired soon after with an excellent record of 26 wins in 27 bouts.

NATIONALITY	WEIGHT(S) FOUGHT	NO. OF FIGHTS	WON–LOST (KO'S)	HONOURS
Nigerian/ British	Heavyweight	27	26-1	WBC heavyweight champion 1992-94 Penta-Continental champion 1993-94 British heavyweight champion 1993 WBO heavyweight champion 1994-95

Larry Holmes

NATIONALITY	WEIGHT(S) FOUGHT	NO. OF FIGHTS	WON–LOST (KO's)	HONOURS
American	Heavyweight	70	65-5 (42)	WBC heavyweight champion 1978-83 IBF heavyweight champion 1983-85

LARRY Holmes was one of the finest heavyweight champions the sport has produced but had the misfortune to box in the post-Muhammad Ali period and lived in the shadow of the 'Greatest'.

Holmes, born in Georgia on 3 November 1949, first came to fame as one of Ali's principle sparring partners after he had failed to make the 1972 Olympic team. During his time with the former three-time world heavyweight champion, Holmes, too, developed a superb damaging left jab and became the consummate boxer.

His professional career took off in 1978 when he beat the dangerous Earnie Shavers on points over 12 rounds to earn himself a shot at Ken Norton's WBC title three months later. The fight was an epic struggle with both boxers level going into the 15th and final round. Holmes was adjudged to have won the round on the scorecard of two judges, and Norton's reign was at an end.

Holmes then won 11 of his first 12 defences by knockout, the 12th being the much-hyped showdown with 'great white hope' Gerry Cooney. This was the most anticipated heavyweight tussle since the Ali-Joe Frazier bouts and ended with the challenger being pulled out of the fight by his corner in the 13th round.

But, in 1985, with Holmes just one fight away from equalling Rocky Marciano's 49-0 record, he met light-heavyweight champ Michael Spinks and lost on points. Holmes also lost the rematch and announced his retirement.

He made abortive comebacks to the ring, losing to Mike Tyson, Evander Holyfield and Oliver McCall but, despite being in his late 40s, was still boxing in the late 1990s.

Evander Holyfield

THE man from Alabama has rarely been out of the headlines in his boxing career. Born on 19 October 1962, Evander Holyfield went from being an unlucky fighter at the 1984 Olympics to heavyweight champion of the world. During those Los Angeles games Holyfield floored opponent Kevin Barry but the referee had given a command to break and he was subsequently disqualified.

He turned pro soon after, fighting and winning an epic battle against WBA cruiserweight champion Dwight Qawi. After securing the IBF and WBA cruiserweight titles, the self-styled 'Real Deal' moved up to heavyweight. In 1990 he knocked out 'Buster' Douglas to win the undisputed heavyweight crown. After defending against George Foreman, Bert Cooper and Larry Holmes, he lost to Riddick Bowe, but won the rematch to lift the WBA and IBF titles. After losing to Michael Moorer he was advised to retire due to a heart defect.

Early in 1995 Holyfield was given a clean bill of health and returned to the ring to win his most famous battle, causing one of the all-time upsets in the process, on 9 November 1996. Rated as a no-hoper by the bookies, Evander outpunched, outboxed and outclassed 'Iron' Mike Tyson to secure the WBA heavyweight championship of the world and a place in boxing history.

Holyfield (right) against Bowe, November 1992.

NATIONALITY	WEIGHT(S) FOUGHT	NO. OF FIGHTS	WON–LOST (KO's)	HONOURS
American	Cruiserweight, heavyweight	36	33-3 (24)	WBA cruiserweight champion 1987-88 IBF cruiserweight champion 1987-88 WBC cruiserweight champion 1988 WBC, WBA and IBF heavyweight champion 1990-92 WBA and IBF heavyweight champion 1993-94

Lloyd Honeyghan

NATIONALITY	WEIGHT(S) FOUGHT	NO. OF FIGHTS	WON–LOST (KO's)	HONOURS
Jamaican	Welterweight, light-middleweight	48	43-5	British welterweight champion 1983-86 European champion 1985-86 Commonwealth champion 1985-86 World welterweight champion 1986 WBC and IBF champion 1986-87 WBC champion 1988-89 Commonwealth light-middleweight champion 1993-94

JAMAICAN-BORN Lloyd Honeyghan (born 22 April 1960), the British, Commonwealth and European welterweight champion, became an overnight sensation worldwide when, on 27 September 1986 in Atlantic City, he stopped undisputed world champion Don Curry of America.

Honeyghan, an aggressive, non-stop fighter, was entirely written off beforehand but his style was exactly what was required to topple a champion beset by weight problems. Backing Curry up from the opening bell, the challenger drained away his opponent's resolve with driving attacks before a cut, caused by a clash of heads, rescued his beaten opponent from further punishment after six rounds.

Continuing to confound his critics, the flamboyant 'Honey' totted up three successful defences of the WBC/IBF versions of his title, including a 40-second annihilation of American danger man Gene Hatcher in Marbella, Spain.

However, domestic and political problems were to prove Honeyghan's downfall. Taking a stance against apartheid, he relinquished his WBA crown in 1986 rather than defend against South African Harold Volbrecht and, with his personal life splashed across the tabloids, lost the WBC version to Jorge Vaca the following year. He was also stripped of the IBF championship as the 12-round schedule was less than their mandatory 15.

Five months later, refocussed and better prepared, Honeyghan knocked out Vaca and held the title for almost a year, when he was stopped in nine rounds by Marlon Starling. His best days behind him, he challenged WBA champion Mark Breland in London in early 1990 but was humiliated in three rounds. A comeback at light-middleweight in 1993 saw Honeyghan take the Commonwealth title, but he is best remembered as the man who throttled the 'Cobra' on that magical night in 1986.

Maurice Hope

THOUGH born on the Caribbean island of Antigua in 1951, Maurice 'Mo' Hope always regarded England as 'the country that made me'. His ambitions gathered momentum in 1973 when the British Boxing Board of Control at last introduced an official light-middleweight category at 11 stone. It meant that he could fight opponents of equal stature rather than have to lose the pounds to reach welterweight or compete against heavier fighters in the middleweight division. When he did fight for the British middleweight crown in June 1975, he was up against the heavier Bunny Sterling, whose bulk was enough to absorb even Mo's hardest left hook.

However, it was a different story when he fought Vito Antuofermo, similar in size to himself, for the European title in Rome in 1976, and the contest was stopped in the 15th in Mo's favour. His dream of winning the world light-middleweight title foundered a year later against German Eckhardt Dagge, who retained his crown after a controversial decision. Two years later he tackled new champ, Italian-Australian Rocky Mattioli, and after flooring his opponent in the first round won in the eighth when Rocky withdrew. Mo successfully defended his crown on three occasions, against American Mike Baker in September 1979, Mattioli again and Argentinian Carlos Herrera.

His final defence was against Puerto Rican Wilfred Benitez — who'd made history as the youngest-ever winner of the world light-welterweight championship — in Las Vegas in May 1981. The young pretender knocked the southpaw Hope down in the 10th and landed the killer punch in the 12th, leaving Hope on his back and motionless in the ring for a full four minutes. Though he should have been stretchered off, the dethroned champ proudly, albeit unsteadily, left the ring upright.

After an unsuccessful crack for the European title in March 1982 against Luigi Minchello, Mo bowed out gracefully.

OVERLEAF: Maurice Hope in action.

NATIONALITY	WEIGHT(S) FOUGHT	NO. OF FIGHTS	WON–LOST (KO's)	HONOURS
Antiguan/ British	Middleweight, light-middleweight	TO COME	TO COME	TO COME

BRY

TLE

James J. Jeffries

NATIONALITY
American
WEIGHT(S) FOUGHT
Heavyweight
NO. OF FIGHTS
21
WON–LOST (KO's)
18-1-2
HONOURS
World heavy-weight champion 1899-1905

JAMES Jackson Jeffries is best remembered for a single blemish on his professional record than for being one of the most formidable heavy-weight champions of all time.

Ohio-born on 15 April 1875 Jeffries, also known as the 'Boilermaker', was a beast of a man, standing at 6ft 2in tall and weighting 215lb. He turned professional in 1896 after moving to California and his first bout was a success, knocking out the ageing Hank Griffin in 14 rounds.

Further victories over Peter Jackson, Tom Sharkey and Joe Goddard set him up for a title at Bob Fitzsimmons' world title in 1899. It was Fitzsimmons' first defence, but he had largely been inactive since his victory over James J Corbett and Jeffries knocked him out in 11 rounds in his 13th professional bout.

Jeffries was to rule the heavy-weight scene for a further six years, dismissing Sharkey twice and knocking out Jack Finnegan in just 55 seconds of the first round. The KO is still the fastest in any heavy-weight title bout.

He retired undefeated in 1905 and was only persuaded to return to the ring after Jack Johnson defeated Tommy Burns to become world champion. Johnson's tenure was seen as an affront by white bigots and big money was offered to Jeffries to fight him.

Despite a courageous performance, the brilliant Johnson was a far superior boxer and stopped Jeffries in 15 rounds at Reno in 1910. Jeffries wisely retired for good this time with an impressive record of 18-1-2.

Ingemar Johansson

INGEMAR Jens Johansson was propelled to international stardom when he overturned the formbook by beating Floyd Patterson to become the heavyweight champion of the world.

Johansson was born on 16 October 1932 in Gothenburg, Sweden, and was an amateur member of the European Golden Gloves team in 1951 and the Swedish Olympic team a year later. He won the European heavyweight title in 1956 and two years later he dramatically moved himself up the world rankings by scoring a one-round knockout over the destructive and formidable Eddie Machin.

The affable, big blond was a promoter's dream and he was booked to challenge Patterson for the world title in New York. Patterson was the overwhelming favourite, but Johansson had not bothered to read the script and despatched his opponent in three rounds.

However, his hold on the title last just one year, for in 1960 Patterson became the first man to win back his heavyweight title by scoring a five-round knockout, again in New York.

A rematch was always on the cards and the next year Johansson and Patterson met at Miami Beach. The Swede looked the more dangerous until, in the sixth round, the famous Patterson combination resulted in his opponent failing to beat the count for a second time.

Johansson won the European heavyweight title in 1962, defended it successfully once and then retired for good. From 1952 to 1963, he had 28 bouts, winning 26 (17 by knockout) — the only losses in his pro career were against Patterson. Johansson later made his residence in west Florida.

NATIONALITY	WEIGHT(S) FOUGHT	NO. OF FIGHTS	WON–LOST (KO'S)	HONOURS
Swedish	Heavyweight	28	26-2	European heavyweight champion 1956-59, 1962-63 World champion 1959-60

Jack Johnson

JOHN Arthur Johnson (born 31 March 1878) was probably one of the finest heavyweight champions ever, but is best remembered for being the first black man to win the world title. Texas-born Johnson, also known as Li'l Artha, became a symbol of hate for white supremacists after he captured the world title with a 15-round annihilation of Tommy Burns in Sydney in 1908.

A superb counter-puncher with the reflexes of a tiger, Johnson was outspoken and became a role model for blacks who, at that time, were supposed to know their place in society . . . and it was not at the top!

A cry went out for a 'great white hope' and former champion James J. Jeffries was — with the aid of an $80,000 purse — persuaded to come out of retirement to fight the great man. But Jeffries was no match for Johnson and he was knocked out in 15 bloody rounds. The result produced race riots across the States that left 11 dead and many hundreds injured.

Having failed to beat Johnson in the ring, the authorities found him guilty under the Mann Act of transporting a woman across the state line. The woman was his fiancée and they were both married after the trial.

But such was the hatred for Johnson, that he fled first to Canada and then to Europe where he successfully defended his title three times in Paris before agreeing to fight Jess Willard in Cuba.

So in 1915, and at 37, Johnson lost his title by way of a 26-round knockout, although many believed he threw the fight in a bid to get on with his life.

LEFT: Johnson (right) still active in his 50s.

NATIONALITY	WEIGHT(S) FOUGHT	NO. OF FIGHTS	WON–LOST (KO's)	HONOURS
American	Heavyweight	114	80-34-45	World heavy-weight champion 1908-15

Roy Jones Jnr

THE term 'best in the world pound-for-pound' is much over-used, but one applied justifiably to American superstar Roy Jones Jnr (born on 16 January 1969 in Pensacola, Florida).

Robbed of Olympic gold in 1988 by a ridiculous decision, two-time Golden Gloves champion Jones made up for his disappointment by moving into the pro ranks and going four years before being taken the distance, the durable Reggie Miller and former world welterweight champion Jorge Vaca among his knockout victims. Jones at last got his world title shot and duly outclassed Bernard Hopkins in 1993 for the vacant IBF middleweight championship.

Quickly moving up to super-middle, Jones took on the notorious James Toney and gave the unbeaten IBF champion — held in many boxing circles as the world's most complete fighter — the ultimate boxing lesson, winning by a landslide margin.

Subsequent stoppage defeats of Antoine Byrd, Vinny Pazienza, Tony Thornton and Merqui Sosa brought tributes to his skill from far and wide. Quick, accurate and devastating with both hands, Jones's ability to finish an ailing opponent is both awesome and conclusive.

Jones, running out of opponents and increasingly content to do just enough to win, moved up to win the WBC light-heavyweight crown in 1996 but his unblemished 34-fight record was sensationally ended in March 1997 when he was disqualified for hitting challenger Montell Griffin, beginning to wilt after nine rounds, while he was down. However, Jones will be determined to put the record straight and only a brave man would bet against him doing so in the future.

NATIONALITY	WEIGHT(S) FOUGHT	NO. OF FIGHTS	WON–LOST (KO's)	HONOURS
American	Middleweight, super-middleweight, light-heavyweight	34	34-0 (29)	IBF middleweight champion 1993-94 IBF super-middleweight champion 1994-

Jake LaMotta

ONE of the true legends of the ring, the 'Bronx Bull' was also one of the toughest and his feats in the ring were mirrored by an equally colourful personal life.

Born on 10 July 1921 on the Lower East Side of New York, LaMotta's teenage delinquency landed him in reform school where, like others, he found his salvation in pugilism. He won the Diamond Belt as an amateur and turned pro in 1941.

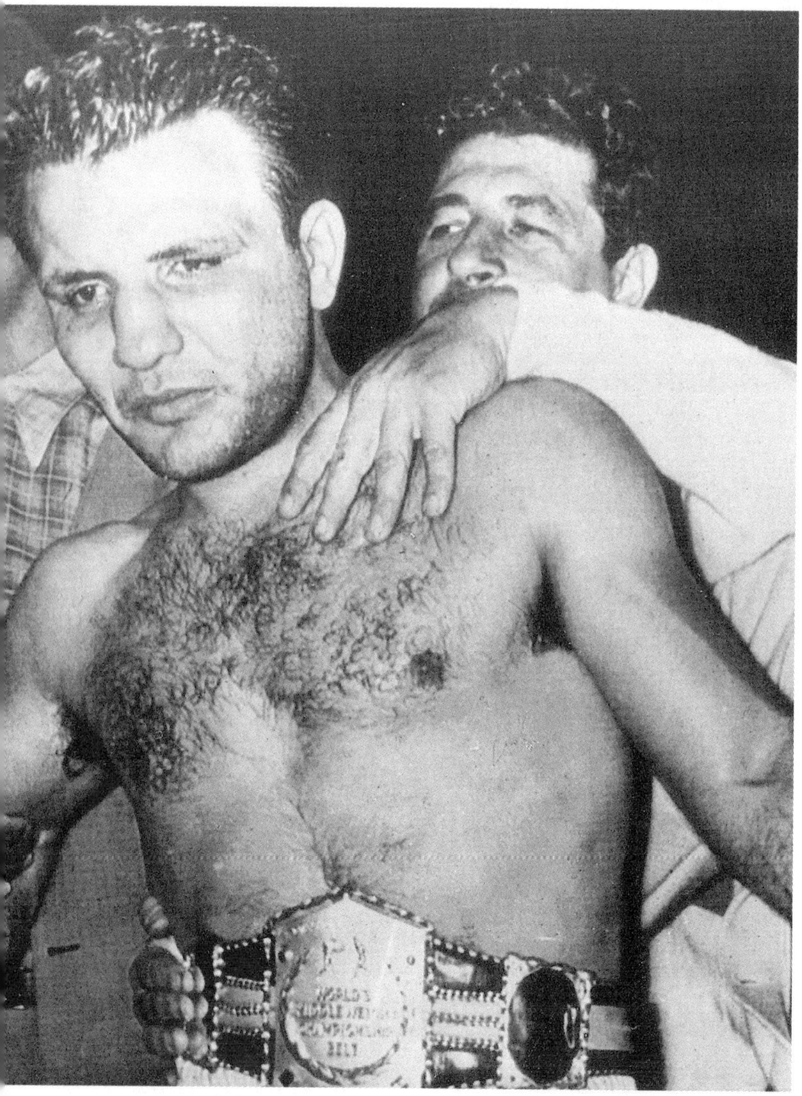

NATIONALITY	WEIGHT(S) FOUGHT	NO. OF FIGHTS	WON–LOST (KO's)	HONOURS
American	Middleweight	106	83-19-4 (30)	World middleweight champion 1949-51

He met Sugar Ray Robinson a total of six times — he was defeated in his first bout with the 'genius' but a rematch on 5 February 1943 gave LaMotta his greatest moment when he knocked Robinson through the ropes and outpointed him, bringing the latter's run of 40 consecutive victories to an end. Robinson, however, beat the 'Bull' in all of their subsequent four meetings.

Despite his superhuman reputation, LaMotta found it difficult to get title fights and only when he agreed to take a dive in the bout against Billy Fox in New York in November 1947 was he given the opportunity to have a go at the world middleweight crown.

He challenged the then-current holder, Frenchman Marcel Cerdan, on 16 June 1949. It was a closely-contested match between two human battering rams but victory was Jake's in the 10th round when Cerdan retired with a hurt shoulder.

LaMotta successfully defended his crown, firstly outpointing Italian Tibero Mitri in New York in July 1950 and then again in the September in Detroit against Frenchman Laurent Dauthille. Dauthille was a real match for the Bull and it looked like he'd wrest the title from LaMotta. But in an exciting 15th round with the Frenchman dominating the game, Jake KO'd the contender with just 13 seconds of the bout left.

He wasn't so lucky when Sugar Ray challenged him in Chicago in February 1951. Robinson's skills saw him through against LaMotta's fearsome strength and the ref stopped the fight in the 13th.

It marked the end of an era. LaMotta retired after a few more defeats, but his achievements were later immortalised in Martin Scorcese's film *Raging Bull* where Robert de Niro successfully played the boxer.

Sugar Ray Leonard

LEONARD was fighter who combined artistry, invention, power and speed but who had a huge ego to match that dazzling array of talent. He was also a canny businessman who reputedly earned $45 million during the heyday of his career.

Born in Wilmington, South Carolina, on 17 May 1956, Sugar Ray came to prominence when he won the gold medal at the 1976 Montreal Olympics. Back in the USA, he took to a professional career like a duck to water and apparently earned $2 million before he ever fought a championship.

His first title was the WBC welterweight which he wrested from Wilfred Benitez in Las Vegas in November 1979. Leonard successfully defended the title against England's Dave 'Boy' Green four months later but lost to Panamanian Roberto Duran in a memorable fight in June 1980. It was a hideous clash of wills with Duran constantly goading his opponent with insults. It was his first defeat in 28 bouts but undeterred he demanded a swift re-match and, using similar psychological methods as Duran had in their first pairing, won back the crown in New Orleans in the November.

On 25 June 1981 Leonard won the WBA light-middleweight title with a KO against Ayub Kalule in Houston, Texas, and then moved up a division to win the WBA welterweight three months later, with reigning champ Thomas Hearns looking like he'd hold on to his crown until a late rally from Ray stopped him in the 14th. Having successfully defended the title against Bruce Finch, he was forced into retirement with a detached left retina.

However he was nagged by the desire to challenge WBC middleweight legend Marvin Hagler and, against medical advice, Sugar Ray finally met his nemesis on 6 April 1987 in Las Vegas. It was a tough but unforgettable bout, pitching Leonard's nimble artistry up against Hagler's brutality. Despite Hagler getting in more punches than his dancing opponent, Leonard did enough to convince the judges on a split decision to give him the match and the title.

This proved to be the last major highlight of his stunning career — Leonard beat Canadian Donny Lalonde to win both WBC super-middleweight and light-heavyweight titles in nine rounds, then proceeded to fight at super-middleweight drawing and beating old rivals Thomas Hearns and Robert Duran respectively, before bowing out of the ring with a defeat at the hands of Terry Norris in 1991. He returned again in 1997, now past 40.

NATIONALITY	WEIGHT(S) FOUGHT	NO. OF FIGHTS	WON–LOST (KO's)	HONOURS
American	Welterweight, light-middleweight, welterweight, middleweight, super-middleweight, light-heavyweight	39 (to 1991)	36-2-1 (25)	WBC welterweight champion 1979-80 WBA light-middleweight champion 1981 Undisputed welterweight champion 1981 WBA middleweight champion 1987 WBC super-middleweight champion 1988-91 WBC light-heavyweight champion 1988-91

Lennox Lewis

BORN on 2 September 1962, Lewis may now be the man with the best chance of unifying the heavyweight crown. Sceptics may label him the boxer who won his first WBC title by picking it out of a rubbish bin after it had been dumped there by Riddick Bowe — but there is no doubt in recent times that fighters from the other heavyweight divisions have done their best to stay outside of the ring where Lennox Lewis is concerned.

Though born in London, Lewis moved with his family to Canada and went on to win gold under that country's flag at the 1988 Olympic Games. Turning pro the following year Lewis punched his way through every opponent placed in front of him. Though he dispatched the likes of Jean Chanet, Mike Weaver and Gary Mason, there were still doubts over his ability to take a punch.

The big test came against Donovan 'Razor' Ruddock at Earl's Court in 1992. Ruddock was a feared man, and only Lewis would step into the ring with him at the time. The experts all said it would be over quickly — and it was, in just 3min 46sec. Yet the experts went with the wrong man as Lewis won a sensational victory.

After beating Frank Bruno in the clash of the Britons, Lewis suffered his only setback, losing his title to a sucker punch from Oliver McCall. But he recovered to take the belt back from a clearly unstable McCall in 1997. Now the biggest opponent facing Lennox Lewis could be a political one. But if he gets his chance in the ring, this man could be the boxer to restore true unity and greatness to the heavyweight division.

NATIONALITY	WEIGHT(S) FOUGHT	NO. OF FIGHTS	WON–LOST (KO's)	HONOURS
Swedish	Heavyweight	28	26-2	European heavyweight champion 1956-59, 1962-63 World champion 1959-60

Charles 'Sonny' Liston

THE life and career of Charles 'Sonny' Liston is shrouded with mystery and controversy, but at his peak he was an awesome champion.

Liston was born the son of an Arkansas sharecropper who fathered 25 children, 13 with Sonny's mother, before he ran away from home at the age of 13. He served two spells in prison for armed robbery, and it was while incarcerated that Liston learned to box. Although he gave his birthdate as 8 May 1932, there is evidence that he began his ring career as early as 1934 at the age of 17. If true, he was 45 years old when he demolished Floyd Patterson to become world champion.

Liston had awesome power: standing 6ft 1in and weighing 215lb, he owned a prodigious left jab and tore through the heavyweight division. He bowled over Cleveland 'Big Cat' Williams, Nino Valdes, Zora Folley and outpointed the equally menacing Eddie Machen.

Against manager Cus D'Amato's advice, champion Patterson fought him in 1962 and was knocked out in the first round. The rematch went the same way 10 months later and Liston was — if not popular with the public — a feared and respected title holder.

But all that changed when a young, brash Cassius Clay debunked his seemingly impregnable myth with a seven-round stoppage two years later in Miami. The return lasted just one round, and critics are still divided over whether Liston took a dive — it's quite possible that he did.

Liston fought on until his body was found in December 1970 — he had been dead for over a week from an alleged drugs' overdose. But his record of 50-4, with 39 KOs, remains uncontested.

NATIONALITY	WEIGHT(S) FOUGHT	NO. OF FIGHTS	WON–LOST (KO's)	HONOURS
American	Heavyweight	54	50-4 (39)	World heavyweight champion 1962-64

Joe Louis

NATIONALITY	WEIGHT(S) FOUGHT	NO. OF FIGHTS	WON–LOST (KO's)	HONOURS
American	Heavyweight	70	67-3-0 (53)	World heavy-weight champion 1937-49

JOSEPH Louis Barrow held the heavyweight crown for the longest period in the history of the sport and challenges Muhammad Ali for the right to be called the 'Greatest'. The 'Brown Bomber', as he became known, defended his title 25 times between 1937 and 1949 when he retired. If it had not been for the Second World War, he would have made many more defences.

Louis was born in Alabama on 13 May 1914, the seventh of nine children, and moved to Detroit when his mother remarried after his father had been committed to a mental institution. He won the US Amateur Athletic Union 175lb championship in 1934 and turned pro the same year.

Louis then knocked out six former heavyweight champs before being knocked out himself by Germany's Max Schmeling in 12 rounds, the first of only three losses as a professional. He claimed the world title by knocking out James J. Braddock in eight rounds in Chicago.

But Louis became a hero when he floored Schmeling in the rematch in one round to rubbish Nazi Propaganda Minister Josef Goebbels' claim that Schmeling was an Aryan superman.

He defended his title seven times in 1941, but after the war was less active and retired long enough for Ezzard Charles to be recognised as his successor. Louis lost a 15-round decision to Charles in 1950 and was then knocked out in eight rounds by future champion Rocky Marciano.

Louis did not manage his financial affairs well and ended up as a greeter for Caesar's Palace in Las Vegas, but his record of 67-3 will stand the test of time and his quiet dignity did much for racial harmony.

Oliver McCall

OLIVER McCall caused one of the biggest upsets in boxing history when he KO'd WBC heavyweight champ Lennox Lewis in September 1994. McCall was an American outsider with no real track record who'd been a sparring partner to the legends including Frank Bruno, Mike Tyson and Lennox Lewis. Having defeated the latter, McCall defended his crown successfully against seasoned campaigner Larry Holmes and was then lined up to meet people's favourite Frank Bruno at Wembley on 2 September 1995.

It was to be big Frank's first match since his ignominious defeat at the hands of Lennox Lewis in Cardiff in October 1993. The British public had hoped Bruno would remain safely in retirement, but the Londoner was determined to have one last pop at a title. Switching managers to Frank Warren, he was granted his wish.

Bruno got off to a good start, building up the points with some good left jabs, yet though McCall got back into the fight by the fifth the pro-Bruno audience showed more life than the boxers! Bruno kept his points lead, and it was up to McCall to launch a final counter-attack to KO the Brit, who received a battering from the desperate American. But Bruno held firm, using all his savvy and reserves to survive. the night finally belonged to Bruno but his reign was short-lived — he lost the crown to Mike Tyson six months later.

McCall's career subsequently nosedived and he allegedly fell prey to drug addiction — a rematch with Lennox Lewis in early 1997 should never have been allowed with the American, recently out of rehabilitation, a passive, weeping wreck in the ring.

NATIONALITY	WEIGHT(S) FOUGHT	NO. OF FIGHTS	WON–LOST (KO's)	HONOURS
American	Heavyweight	Detailed stats not available	Detailed stats not available	WBC heavyweight champion 1994-95

Michael McCallum

NATIONALITY	WEIGHT(S) FOUGHT	NO. OF FIGHTS	WON–LOST (KO'S)	HONOURS
Jamaican	Light-middleweight, middleweight, light-heavyweight	54	49-4-1 (36)	WBA light-middleweight champion 1984-87 WBA middleweight champion 1988-917 WBC light-heavyweight champion 1994-95

BORN in Kingston, Jamaica, on 7 December 1956, Mike McCallum became known as the 'Bodysnatcher' on account of his fearsome body punching. Indeed he holds the record for the most punches landed in one round, connecting 93 blows in the fifth round of his fight against Nicky Walker in October 1991.

McCallum came to prominence at the Commonwealth Games held in his native Jamaica in 1978 by winning the welterweight gold medal: he turned pro three years later and won 21 fights in a row to face Irishman Sean Mannion for the vacant WBA light-middleweight crown in 1984. In a close contest, McCallum outpointed his opponent and went on to successfully defend his title over three years against the likes of Don Curry (a one-blow KO) and Julian Jackson.

He then stepped up to the middleweight division and he eventually won the vacant WBA title in 1989 against Herol Graham. Two years later,

however, McCallum had the title taken away when he agreed to fight James Toney, the IBF champion — the contest ended in a draw.

Subsequently he moved up to light-heavyweight and won the WBC title from Jeff Harding in 12 rounds on 23 July 1994 at Bismarck, North Dakota. He then lost this in his second defence to Fabrice Tiozzo in Lyon in June 1995, making another challenge to regain the belt in November 1996; this again ended in defeat, this time by Roy Jones.

Gerald McClellan

GERALD McClellan was one of the most ferocious fighters of his era, but his career came to an abrupt end on the night of 25 February 1995 at the fists of Nigel Benn, the 'Dark Destroyer'.

Born in Freeport, Illinois, McClellan quickly established himself as a fighting machine, with a formidable record: he despatched 29 of his first 31 opponents, 20 of them within the first round!

McClellan wrested the WBC middleweight crown from Julian Jackson on 8 May 1993 in Las Vegas, destroying the champ in just five rounds. He then successfully defended his new status against Jay Bell and Gilbert Baptist, before he and Jackson enjoyed a re-match. This time, it only took McClellan a single round to KO his rival on 7 May 1994.

Gerald then relinquished the crown to move up a division to super-middleweight and immediately signalled his intent by challenging Essex boy Nigel Benn, some four years his senior, for a crack at the WBC world title. The date was duly was set for a bout the London Arena, where the two met before a capacity 12,000-strong audience.

Now a seasoned 31-year old, Benn saw himself as a more controlled fighter who'd learnt the wisdom of survival. It proved to be a brutal match: indeed, Benn looked like he'd go out in the first round when McClellan knocked him through the ropes and into the ring! The American rained down punch after punch at Benn but he defiantly took the punishment, much to his opponent's surprise.

Benn was floored again in the eighth but at the count of eight he managed to get back into the fight and landed a well-connected right hook in McClellan's face. The spirit seemed to ebb out of the American from this point and halfway through round 10 he sank to down to be counted out. The underdog had won, but it proved to be a something of a Pyrrhic victory when it was discovered that Gerald McClellan was suffering from something worse than just post-fight fatigue. He was eventually taken to hospital where doctors had to operate on a blood clot — and, though this was successfully removed, McClellan suffered from permanent brain damage. His ring career was over.

NATIONALITY
American
WEIGHT(S) FOUGHT
Middleweight, super-middleweight
NO. OF FIGHTS
Detailed stats not available
WON–LOST (KO's)
Detailed stats not available
HONOURS
WBC middleweight champion 1993-94

Barry McGuigan

NATIONALITY	WEIGHT(S) FOUGHT	NO. OF FIGHTS	WON–LOST (KO's)	HONOURS
Irish	Featherweight	35	32-3	British and European featherweight champion 1983-85 WBA featherweight champion 1985-86

FINBAR Patrick McGuigan, born on 28 February 1961 and more commonly known as Barry, helped unite a troubled country when in 1985 he took the WBA world featherweight title back to Ireland after beating long-time champion Eusebio Pedroza at a swelling Queens Park Rangers football ground in Shepherd's Bush, London.

McGuigan had enjoyed a distinguished amateur career before thrilling crowds at the King's Hall, Belfast, with his rise to a world title fight. An aggressive, all-action fighter, he won the Commonwealth gold medal in 1978 at bantamweight before a surprising early defeat in the 1980 Olympics.

Turning professional the following year, he overcame another early defeat and the subsequent death of one of his opponents, Nigerian Young Ali, to win the British featherweight title in 1983 and the vacant European crown the same year. But his greatest night arrived on 8 June 1985, when he floored Panamanian Eusebio Pedroza, who had successfully defended his title 19 times, before winning on points.

McGuigan held the title for two defences before taking an ill-judged match in June 1986 with late substitute Steve Cruz in Las Vegas. Clearly uncomfortable in the searing heat, McGuigan was beaten on points, his Texan opponent far better suited to the conditions. There followed an acrimonious battle with manager Barney Eastwood, which kept him out of the ring while he should have been in his prime. A return at super-featherweight was disrupted by a cuts defeat to Jim McDonnell, and he retired.

McGuigan's must be considered an unfulfilled talent. His swarming attacks and murderous body punches were world-class and his record of 32 wins from 35 fights, 28 inside the distance, bears the closest inspection.

Duke McKenzie

A member of one of the UK's most notorious fighting dynasties, Duke was born in Croydon, Surrey, on 5 May 1963 and enjoyed a highly successful career in four divisions, in three of which he was a champion. Turning professional in 1982, he set his sights on the British flyweight title, which he won in 1985, adding the European belt to his roster in May 1986 by conquering WBC champ Charlie Magri.

In October 1988, he KO'd Rolando Bohol at Wembley in the 11th round to win his first world title, the IBF flyweight crown. After one successful defence against American Tony DeLuca, he lost the title to Dave McAuley in June 1989, and responded by moving up to bantamweight. Outpointed by Frenchman Thierry Jacob in a bid for the European crown, Duke sprang back with a bid for the WBO world bantamweight title in what was to be the greatest fight of his career.

Scheduled for the Elephant & Castle Leisure Centre in South London on 30 June 1991, Duke was up against 'streetfighting' Texan Gaby Canizales, who'd wrested the world title from Columbian Miguel Lora just three months before with an amazing display of fist power inside two rounds.

Duke's victory that night, he always maintained, was down to his deep-rooted fear. The Croydonian never let the Texan get near him, constantly jabbing at his face in a contest where skill triumphed over brute force — Duke outpointed the American in nine of the 12 rounds.

After two successful defences against Cesar Soto and Wilfredo Vargas, Rafael Del Valle KO'd him in the first round in London in May 1992. Undeterred, McKenzie then moved up to take the WBO super-bantamweight title from American Jesse Benavides on points in October. He lost his first defence but found success again by winning the British featherweight title in December 1993.

Sadly his bid for a fourth world title against WBO featherweight champ Steve Robinson failed when he was KO'd in the ninth in Cardiff on 1 October 1994.

NATIONALITY	WEIGHT(S) FOUGHT	NO. OF FIGHTS	WON–LOST (KO's)	HONOURS
British	Flyweight, bantamweight, super-bantamweight, featherweight	41	36-5	British flyweight champion 1985-86 European flyweight champion 1986-88 IBF flyweight champion 1988-89 WBO bantamweight champion 1991-92 WBO super-bantamweight champion 1992-93 British featherweight champion 1993-94

Charlie Magri

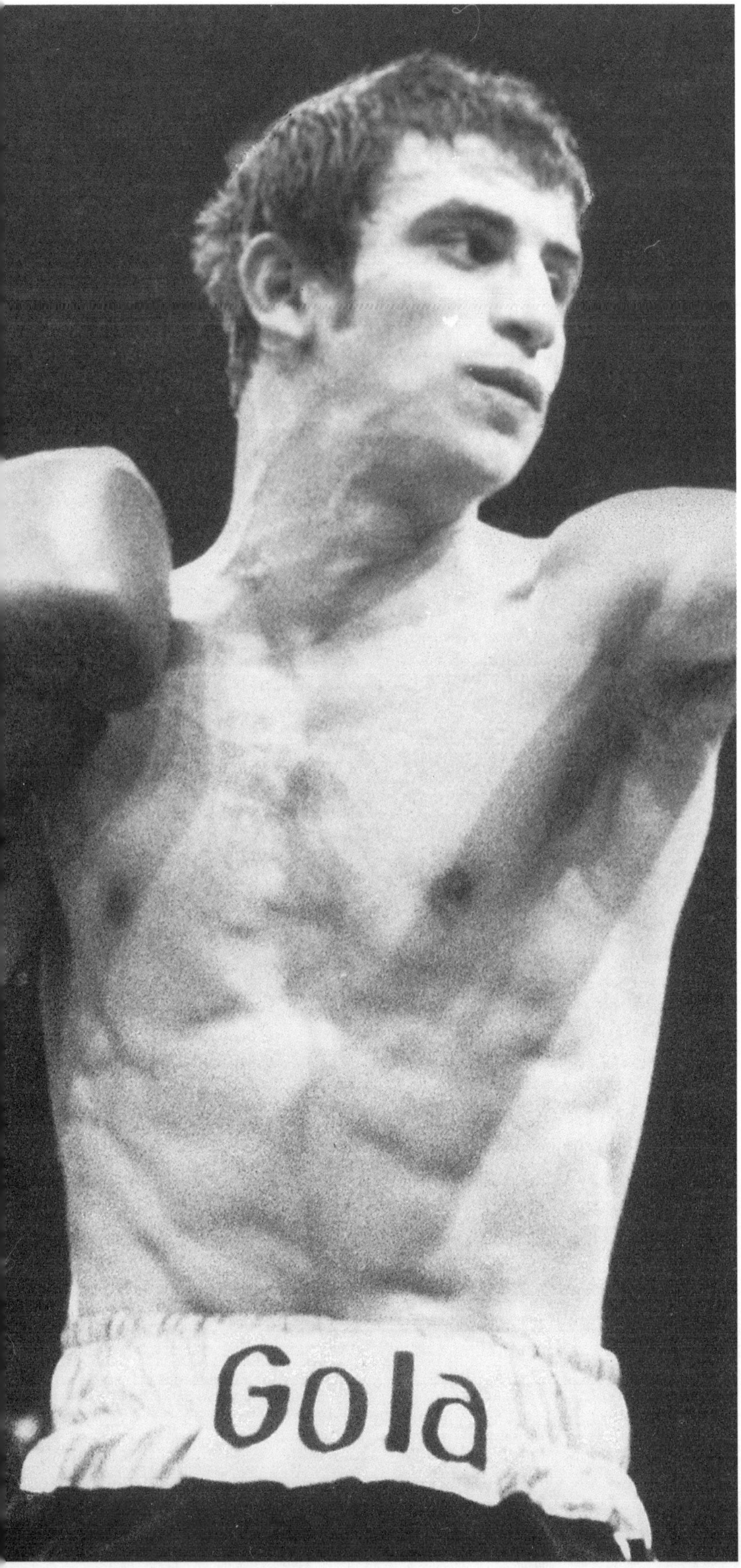

TUNISIAN-BORN (20 July 1956) Charlie Magri looked likely to take the world flyweight scene by storm when, after three successive ABA titles, he joined the professional circuit and won the British flyweight championship in only his third fight.

Magri, handled by shrewd East End manager Terry Lawless, breezed through rival after rival with his blistering speed and crisp punches, but was kept off the world stage to concentrate on the European title, which he tore from ageing Italian Franco Udella in 1979. Stylish as well as powerful, able to score points with every punch in the manual as well as possessing a KO punch, the world seemed Magri's oyster.

Then the wheels fell off. Magri's ability to take punishment, as yet largely untested, came into doubt as he was stopped by unregarded Latin fighters Juan Diaz and Jose Torres. However, Lawless nursed his boy towards a world title shot and on 15 March 1983, at Wembley Arena in London, Magri stayed out of trouble and stopped Eleoncio Mercedes of the Dominican Republic in seven rounds to become WBC world flyweight champion.

Magri's reign was short-lived, Frank Cedeno taking the title in his first defence. He returned to the European scene, where he won, lost and regained the crown before making one last, unsuccessful bid for world glory against Thailand's Sot Chitalada in February 1985. After losing his European title to fellow Briton Duke McKenzie, Magri bowed out with 30 victories from 35 fights and a special place in the hearts of the East London fighting community.

NATIONALITY	WEIGHT(S) FOUGHT	NO. OF FIGHTS	WON–LOST (KO's)	HONOURS
British	Flyweight	35	30-5	British flyweight champion 1977-81 European flyweight champion 1979-82, 1984, 1985-86 WBC flyweight champion 1983

Rocky Marciano

ROCCO Francis Marchegiano (born 1 September 1923) is the only world champion in any division to end his career undefeated. Known as the Rock or the Brockton Blockbuster, Marciano was the oldest of six children born to Italian parents in Brockton, Massachusetts. After a short but promising amateur career, he turned professional two years after the war.

Knockouts of Rex Layne, an ageing Joe Louis, Lee Savold and Harry 'Kid' Matthews earned him the chance to win the world championship. He survived a first-round knock down by holder Jersey Joe Walcott to claim the championship with a 13-round knockout in 1952.

The rematch was much shorter with Marciano despatching Walcott in round one — the 11th first-round knockout of his career. He defended his title successfully against Roland LaStarza and Britain's Don Cockell before two epic battles with former champion Ezzard Charles.

The second bout almost ended Rocky's reign, for his nose was so badly split that the referee was about to stop the contest. But Marciano, whose crouched style had brought him so much success, sprang into action and knocked out Charles in round eight.

Marciano's final defence was against light-heavyweight champion Archie Moore. Again he had to recover from an early knockdown to catch up with the wily Moore in round nine. He announced his retirement shortly afterwards.

Marciano was killed in a plane crash on 31 August 1969, a day before his birthday — ironically, he was on his way to his party, but his record of 49-0 is still unsurpassed.

NATIONALITY	WEIGHT(S) FOUGHT	NO. OF FIGHTS	WON–LOST (KO's)	HONOURS
American	Heavyweight	49	49-0 (43)	Word heavyweight champion 1952-56

Terry Marsh

BORN on 7 February 1958 Terry Marsh enjoyed an unbeaten reign in the ring. His 27 fights saw him win 26 of them, 10 inside the distance, with one draw. Marsh had always intended to walk away from boxing undefeated but in the end it was not the way he would have wished it. The day after signing a contract to defend his title the one-time fireman announced that he was an epileptic, effectively ending his career.

Marsh was a determined, articulate man and was one of the outstanding British amateurs of the 1970s. He secured three ABA titles in four finals before deciding to turn pro in 1981. Marsh had a style all of his own and while his jab and speed of feet approach never made him a massive crowd-puller it was good enough to win him a Lonsdale belt at light-welterweight.

He went on to retain the European title twice in 1986 to move towards a world title bid. When it came it was against Joe Louis Manley — the little known International Boxing Federation champion.

Marsh surprised everyone as he abandoned his previous jab and move approach to hurl himself at his opponent in best streetfighting tradition. This was to win him many new fans and after a successful defence, a mouth-watering clash was set up with Hector 'Macho' Camacho.

Frank Warren negotiated the contract which Marsh signed, only for the news to break about the fighter's medical condition. Terry Marsh tried to have his licence reinstated in 1989 but the Board of Control refused. It was a sad end to a fine career and possibly the full facts of the story will never be known.

NATIONALITY	WEIGHT(S) FOUGHT	NO. OF FIGHTS	WON–LOST (KO's)	HONOURS
British	Light-welter-weight	27	26-0-1	British light-welterweight champion 1984-86 European light-welter-weight champion 1985-86 IBF 1987

Ray Mercer

MUSCULAR Ray Mercer first sprang to prominence at the 1986 Olympic Games in Seoul where, having beaten highly-rated Michael Bentt in the trials, he went on to win the heavyweight gold medal for the USA. Turning pro, Mercer won the WBO heavyweight title five years after Olympic gold by KO'ing Italian Francesco Damiani in the ninth round of his second defence of the crown in Atlantic City.

Mercer successfully defended the title on 18 October of the same year, again in Atlantic City, against Kansas City cowboy Tommy Morrison. This time victory came in the fifth round, but Mercer was later stripped of the honour when he refused to defend the title against the nominated challenger, Michael Moorer.

But perhaps his most dubious claim to fame was when the Manhattan District Attorney's brought a charge of bribery against him after his fight at Madison Square garden on 6 February 1993 against Jesse Ferguson. The latter claimed that he'd been offered a six-figure sum to go down but Mercer was eventually proven innocent. The winner was due a shot at Riddick Bowe, the surprise undisputed heavyweight champ, but sadly for Mercer that prize went to his opponent.

NATIONALITY	WEIGHT(S) FOUGHT	NO. OF FIGHTS	WON–LOST (KO's)	HONOURS
American	Heavyweight	Detailed stats not available	Detailed stats not available	WBO heavyweight champion 1991-92

Freddie Mills

NATIONALITY	WEIGHT(S) FOUGHT	NO. OF FIGHTS	WON–LOST (KO's)	HONOURS
British	Light-heavy-weight	97	74-17-6	British and Empire light-heavyweight champion 1942-50 European light-heavy-weight champion 1947-50 World light-heavyweight champion 1948-50

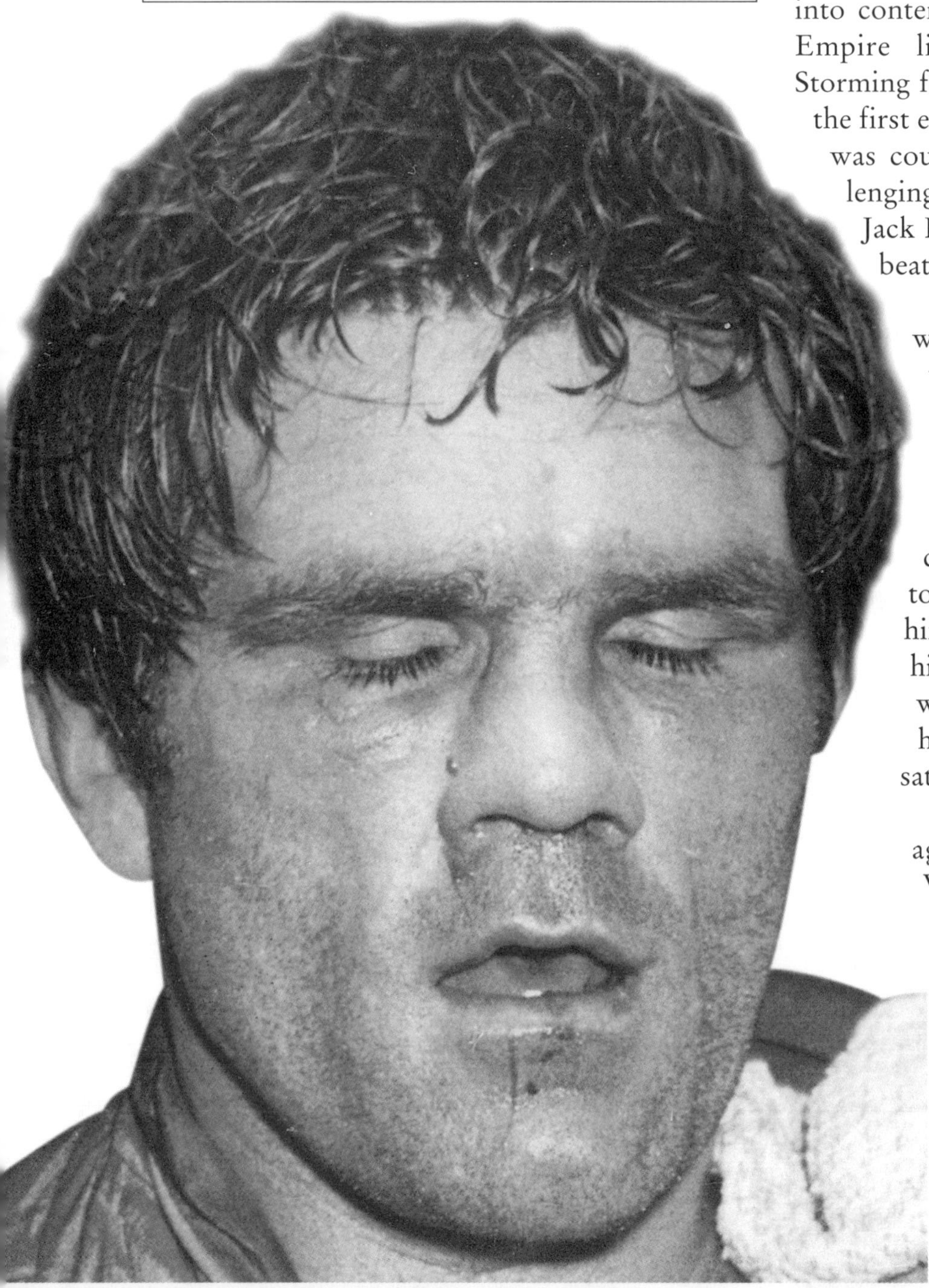

FIGHTING came naturally to Freddie Mills (born on 26 June 1919 in Parkstone), who learned his trade the hard way by taking on all-comers in fairground booths and shrugged off many severe beatings to become light-heavy-weight champion of the world.

Mills, a brawler who could not resist a shot at men far bigger than himself, fought his way into contention for Len Harvey's British and Empire light-heavyweight titles in 1942. Storming forward from the bell, Mills inflicted the first ever knockout on the champion, who was counted out in round two. But, challenging for the heavyweight crown against Jack London two years later, Freddie was beaten on points.

In 1946, Mills returned from his wartime service with the RAF to face world light-heavyweight champion Gus Lesnevich in London and was pummelled to defeat in the 10th. Further batterings, including one at the hands of British heavyweight champion Bruce Woodcock, seemed to suggest Mills' best days were past him but in July 1948 Lesnevich gave him a rematch and the British bulldog was crowned undisputed world light-heavyweight champion after 15 pulsating rounds.

Never one to shirk a fight, Mills again fancied his chances against Woodcock but was stopped in the 14th. In 1950, American Joey Maxim relieved Mills of his world title and he decided to call it a day, later entering the night-club business. Mills was discovered dead of gunshot wounds outside his Soho premises in July 1965, and his death, recorded as suicide, remains a mystery to this day.

Alan Minter

STYLISH southpaw Alan Minter, born on 17 August 1951 in Crawley, England, was hindered by his tendency to cut easily but nevertheless built up an impressive record as he dominated British middleweight boxing in the 1970s, culminating in a six-month spell as world champion in 1980.

Minter, whose accurate jabbing style won him the nickname 'Boom-Boom', turned professional in late 1972 with an ABA title and Olympic bronze medal to his credit, but his early years were dotted with defeats until he outpointed Kevin Finnegan for the vacant British title in 1975. He was to meet — and beat — Finnegan three times in all, every decision narrow and hotly disputed.

European champion in two spells in the late 1970s, Minter relinquished the title to go for world honours. In March 1980, given little chance against Italy's undisputed world champion Vito Antuofermo, Minter won on points in Las Vegas to become the first British fighter since 1915 to win a world title in America. Back in London for the rematch three months later, Antuofermo was knocked out in eight rounds.

But on 27 September of the same year, Minter met his match and the world a formidable new champion in the shape of Marvin Hagler. The American, swarming all over Minter from the opening bell, detonated jabs and right hooks on his stunned opponent, who was badly cut and rescued by the referee in the third.

The appalling crowd scenes which followed shamed British boxing and deprived the country of witnessing Hagler's talents first-hand again. Minter took time to recover from his beating but retired a year later when his bid to win Tony Sibson's European title ended in a thundering third-round knockout.

NATIONALITY	WEIGHT(S) FOUGHT	NO. OF FIGHTS	WON–LOST (KO's)	HONOURS
British	Middleweight	49	39-9-1	British middleweight champion 1975-77, 1977-78 European middleweight champion 1977, 1978-79 World middleweight champion 1980

Archie Moore

ARCHIE Moore's mother claimed he was born on 13 December 1913 but he always insisted it was 1916. The record books cannot confirm which is the correct date but they do show a fight record of 199-26-8 (145 KOs). Moore won the light heavyweight world championship in 1955, aged (at least) 39, and he held the title for more than nine years.

Though nearly every opponent he faced in later life were younger, Moore had tremendous strength and courage, which saw him produce an incredible 145 knockouts. He would be champion for nine years and fifty-five days, the longest ever by a light-heavyweight. The man, literally did not know when he was beaten. A clash with Canadian Yvon Durelle saw Moore knocked down three times in the first round but the American, 42 years old at the time, rallied to win the bout in the 11th.

The only time Moore came unstuck was when he attempted to move up to heavyweight. Twice he challenged champions and twice he was knocked out, one of these KOs coming against Rocky Marciano. Aged 43, Moore fought Floyd Patterson for the vacant world heavyweight title. Patterson, who was just 21 at the time, won the contest in the fifth.

Archie Moore fought for the final time in 1961. He won on points against Giulio Rinaldi but retired soon afterwards. He was stripped of the title in 1962 but returned to the ring three years later for an exhibition match. Depending on who you believed, Moore or his mum, he was now either 52 years of age — or 49.

NATIONALITY	WEIGHT(S) FOUGHT	NO. OF FIGHTS	WON–LOST (KO's)	HONOURS
American	Light-heavy-weight	215	183-22-10	World light-heavyweight champion 1952-62

Michael Moorer

BORN in Monesson Pennsylvania on 12 November 1967, Michael Moorer has become one of the most controversial figures in American boxing since Mike Tyson, his violent behaviour outside the ring — he was convicted for breaking the bones of policemen who'd insulted him — and moody demeanour marring what promised to be a great career.

Moorer sprang to fame as a fast and savage puncher, going on to win the WBO light-heavyweight title in 1988 and successfully defending it a record 10 times in four years. In February 1993, he relinquished his WBO title commenting that it 'was retarding his career'. He then set off on the road to win the coveted world heavyweight title and in doing so again courted controversy. In the run-up to the championship match, he encountered no real leading heavyweight contenders.

The match for the WBA/IBF title was held in Las Vegas on 23 April 1993 against Evander Holyfield. Moorer reputedly started better, but in the second round — judged even by seasoned adjudicator Jerry Roth — Holyfield struck a glancing blow to Moorer's his jaw. The contender's resilience took Holyfield by surprise and subsequent rounds saw Moorer, a southpaw, turn the contest in his favour.

Holyfield's stamina suggested he might yet win the day but there was an extraordinary turnaround after Moorer's trainer, Teddy Atlas, began to bait his protégé with a string of jibes that appeared to rejuvenate him and strengthen his resolve. Moorer's right jab wore down Holyfield's defences and the judgement gave the bruising match to the contender on points.

Moorer was the first left-handed pugilist to have won the title but, rather than defend his hard-won championship against a worthy contestant like Lennox Lewis, chose to defend it against the ageing George Foreman. However when the pair did get to finally slug it in Las Vegas in November 1994, it was the gentlemanly Foreman who turned up trumps!

NATIONALITY	WEIGHT(S) FOUGHT	NO. OF FIGHTS	WON–LOST (KO'S)	HONOURS
American	Light-heavy-weight, heavy-weight	39	38-1 (31)	WBO light-heavyweight champion 1988-91 (92) WBO heavy-weight champion 1992-93 WBA/IBF heavyweight champion 1994

Tommy Morrison

NATIONALITY	WEIGHT(S) FOUGHT	NO. OF FIGHTS	WON–LOST (KO's)	HONOURS
American	Heavyweight	Detailed stats not available	Detailed stats not available	WBO heavy-weight champion 1993

SO legend has it, Kansas City's Tommy 'The Duke' Morrison is the great nephew of one of the cinema's immortals, John Wayne (aka Marion Morrison) Nor do the show biz connections stop there: he also starred in the final Rocky film!

Morrison had first bid for the WBO heavyweight title when he met Ray Mercer in Atlantic City on 18 October 1991 but lost the match when the referee stopped it in the fifth. He got his second crack on 7 June 1993 in Las Vegas when he took on the ageing George Foreman and outpointed him over 12 rounds.

Morrison was then set to face reigning WBC world champ, Lennox Lewis in a tournament in Las Vegas in the spring of 1994. It was a showdown that would make each fighter a cool five million dollars each richer! 'The Duke' however wanted a warm-up - and this was to prove his undoing.

Morrison met Michael Bentt on 29 October 1993 in Tulsa, Oklahoma — Bentt, who enjoyed dual US/UK citizenship, was at the pinnacle of a brilliant career having won all 11 of his professional fights. The prospect of facing Bentt didn't unduly worry Morrison and within seconds of the bell of the first round had landed his fabled left hook on his opponent's jaw. The contender was wobbling and Morrison arrogantly but carelessly moved in for the kill — Bentt saw his chance and hit Morrison's unguarded chin with a right-hander that landed him on the canvas. He got up at the count of eight, but two more volleys from Bentt sent him toppling again and, under the WBO rules, the match was stopped. The title went to Bentt in an incredible 93 seconds!

Morrison later returned to the headlines when he disclosed that he had been tested positive for HIV in February 1996 after his scheduled bout against Arthur Weathers had been cancelled by the Nevada State Athletic Commission.

Ken Norton

BORN on 9 August 1945 in Jacksonville, Illinois, pugnacious Ken Norton's career will always be remembered as one of the finest fighters of the 1970s and for his three unforgettable contests against Muhammad Ali.

Norton won his first 16 fights in a row until he was beaten by Jose Luis Garcia in 1970. It was during a second successful 'roll' — 14 wins in succession — that he first faced Ali. In March 1973 Norton wrested the NABF title from 'the Greatest' in a points win that saw him break Ali's jaw!

Six months later, Ali won the return match on a fair decision. Norton then went up against the formidable George Foreman on 26 March 1974 in Caracas, Venezuela, but his brave bid for the world heavyweight title ended in disaster after only two rounds. Seven straight KOs followed, restoring his confidence, and on 26 September 1976 in New York, Norton met Ali again for the third and final time - it was an extremely close contest but Ali took the verdict.

When Leon Spinks failed to defend his title against Norton in March 1978, the WBC announced him champion on account of his 15-rounds-points victory over Jimmy Young in their final eliminator in Las Vegas the previous November.

Norton failed to retain his crown against Larry Holmes in June 1978 when he was outpointed over 15 rounds, and fought a further five bouts before his retirement in 1981.

NATIONALITY	WEIGHT(S) FOUGHT	NO. OF FIGHTS	WON–LOST (KO's)	HONOURS
American	Heavyweight	50	42-7-1	WBC Heavyweight champion 1978

Floyd Patterson

NATIONALITY	American
WEIGHT(S) FOUGHT	Heavyweight
NO. OF FIGHTS	64
WON–LOST (KO's)	55-8-1 (40)
HONOURS	World heavy-weight champion 1956-59, 1960-62

THOUGH never regarded in quite the same legendary status as an Ali or Marciano, most would agree that Floyd Patterson still possessed the fastest pair of fists in the history of the game.

Born in Waco, North Carolina on 4 January 1935, Patterson spent his formative years as a delinquent on the streets of New York, though at times he could be deeply introverted too. Boxing saved him from a life of crime and he became the protégé of manager Cus D'Amato, who was later associated with Mike Tyson. He would supervise Floyd's subsequent career that boasted 64 bouts, 55 of which he won including 40 KOs. Through it all D'Amato acted as a father figure to this kid from the ghetto.

Patterson's first major success came in 1952 when he won the middleweight gold medal at the Helsinki Olympic Games. His next step was to turn fully pro — all through his subsequent life in the ring, Patterson maintained a physique of around 200lb, in today's terms a cruiserweight. He perfected a combination punching technique which included hitting an opponent with a six-punch volley as he was going down. He also learned to use his leg speed for a new kind of blow, the 'leaping left hook'.

Floyd was soon on the way up, despatching potential superiors Jacques Crecy-Rover and Tommy 'Hurricane' Jackson. The title challenge in 1956 was against Archie Moore, the man who'd once floored Rocky Marciano. Floyd rose regally to the occasion and KO'd Moore with a classic left-hook in the fourth. His first defence was against the aforementioned Jackson whom he'd narrowly outpointed first time around but whom he now destroyed in the 11th. The second was against Peter Rademacher, who'd become the American Olympic heavyweight champion in 1956 and was duly KO'd.

After fights against Texan Roy Harris and Brit Brian London, both safe bets, Patterson eventually met his Waterloo in 1959 at the hands of European champ Ingemar Johansson who knocked him down seven times and the fight was stopped in the third round. Patterson confounded his critics by being the first man to regain the world title, once more against the Swede.

However his record was somewhat tarnished when he lost the defence of the championship to Sonny Liston in 1962 in just one round. Further bids to regain his crown against the likes of Muhammad Ali failed and Floyd retired in 1972.

Sugar Ray Robinson

REAL legends of the ring can be quickly counted but Sugar Ray Robinson, born Walker Smith in Detroit on 3 May 1921, is probably the biggest of them. He lost just 19 times in 202 fights professionally, most of them at the end of his 25-year career, and beat 14 fellow world champions. He also won the world middleweight title an unprecedented five times — a scriptwriter couldn't invent it.

A Golden Gloves champion at featherweight, Robinson borrowed his name from another fighter when he turned up for his first amateur fight unregistered, and never gave it back. Turning pro in 1940, Robinson won 40 straight fights before losing to 'Raging Bull' Jake LaMotta — a defeat he was to avenge on five occasions.

Then came the most astonishing sequence in fight history as Robinson went 91 bouts without defeat, winning and relinquishing the world welterweight title and beating old adversary LaMotta for the middleweight crown in February 1951. A famous reverse against Britain's Randolph Turpin later that year was quickly avenged, while former champion Rocky Graziano fell in three rounds.

Tempted by the lack of worthwhile matches to move up a weight, Robinson fought Joey Maxim for the world light-heavyweight title but, ahead on points, was forced to retire exhausted after 13 rounds. After a brief retirement he was back to regain his middleweight title from Carl Olsen in 1955, then lost and regained it against both Gene Fulmer and Carmen Basilio before losing it for the last time against Paul Pender in January 1960, his 40th year. Financial problems saw him box on until 1965, but Robinson will be recalled by many as the finest ever to grace the ring.

NATIONALITY	WEIGHT(S) FOUGHT	NO. OF FIGHTS	WON–LOST (KO's)	HONOURS
American	Welterweight, middleweight	202	175-19-6 (110)	World welterweight champion 1946-51, World middleweight champion 1951, 1951-2, 1955-57, 1958-60

Barney Ross

BORN Beryl David Rosofsky on 23 December 1909, Barney Ross became world champ in three weights, fighting a total of 81 bouts in a long and distinguished career, during which he enjoyed 73 wins.

Ross grew up in Chicago in the 'roaring 1920s' and turned pro in 1929. He became world lightweight and light-welterweight champ on 23 June 1933 when he outpointed reigning supremo Tony Canzoneri in ten rounds.

The pair met again in the September when Ross successfully defended his lightweight crown — a feat he was to pull off a further seven times until he relinquished the title and moved up to welterweight. In May 1934 he plundered the welterweight title from Jimmy McLarnin outpointing him over 15 rounds. He lost to the Irishman four months later but again beat his rival in a third meeting in New York in May 1935. He then defended his welterweight title twice until fellow American Henry Armstrong beat him on points in New York in May 1938.

This was his last match and he retired to eventually serve as a highly decorated soldier in the US forces during World War II.

NATIONALITY	WEIGHT(S) FOUGHT	NO. OF FIGHTS	WON–LOST (KO's)	HONOURS
American	Lightweight, light-welter-weight, welter-weight	81	73-4-4	World light-weight champion 1933-35 World light-welterweight champion 1933-35 World welter-weight champion 1934, 1935-38

Alan Rudkin

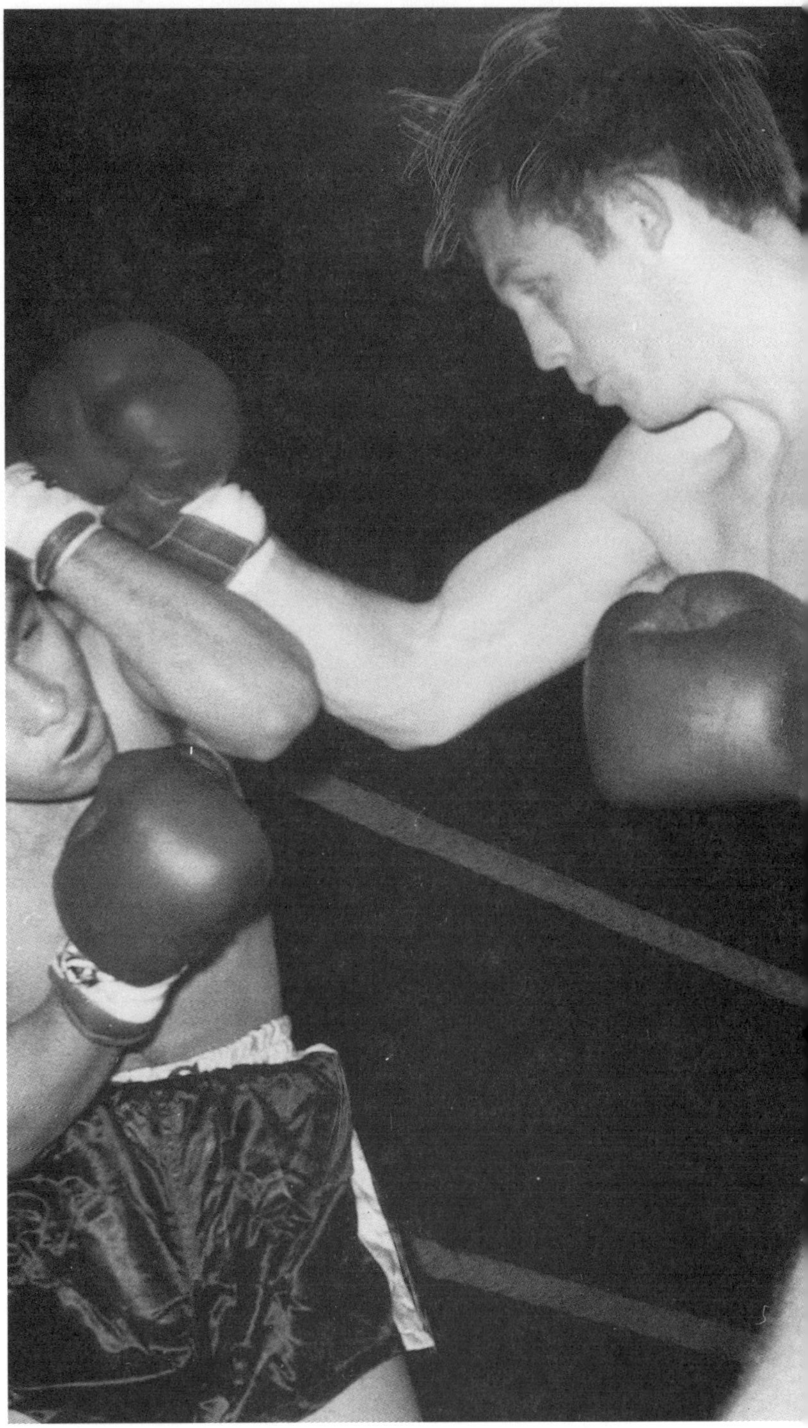

BORN in 1941 in Liverpool. Alan Rudkin was a boxer of great stamina and determination, an angelic-looking little guy who delivered a mean left hook.

Rudkin never quite made it to the top of the bantamweight ladder — he came out of an era that spawned some of the greats such as Irishman Johnny Caldwell from whom he won the British bantamweight title and Scot Walter McGowan. Rudkin was great rivals with the latter — in the first of two full 15-round bouts, McGowan wrested the crown only to have it taken back from him later by the doughty northerner.

In 1966 he went to Japan to compete against Fighting Harada in Tokyo. Rudkin was up against the referee as well as a tough opponent, and lost narrowly on points. Harada eventually lost his title to Australian aborigine Lionel Rose and in 1969 Rudkin travelled to Melbourne to make a further title bid. Once again it was a close call — the Liverpudlian lost the first five rounds and received a bad cut in the third, but courageously stuck with it.

The Aborigine subsequently collapsed in his dressing room with stomach cramps unable to continue while the Englishman looked as fresh as a daisy. Yet one of the judges announced Lionel the winner by an outrageous 15 points and didn't even award him one round.

Rudkin hoped to get another shot at Rose but the Aussie lost the title to Mexican, Ruben Olivares and Alan had to face this lightning-fast puncher in California in December 1969, where the Brit was dispatched with a left hook in just two rounds.

Unfortunately Rudkin began another kind of battle in the final days of his career — one with his weight and he found it hard to adhere to the 8st 6lb limit. In spite of a win against Franco Zurlo for the European title, he retired soon after to run a pub in his hometown.

NATIONALITY	WEIGHT(S) FOUGHT	NO. OF FIGHTS	WON–LOST (KO's)	HONOURS
British	Detailed stats not available	British bantamweight	European bantamweight	Detailed stats not available

Max Schmeling

NATIONALITY	WEIGHT(S) FOUGHT	NO. OF FIGHTS	WON–LOST (KO's)	HONOURS
German	Light-heavy-weight, heavy-weight	70	56-10-4 (38)	World light-heavyweight champion 1927-28 World heavy-weight champion 1930-32 European heavyweight champion 1939

MAX Schmeling, one of the most misjudged pugilists of the 1930s, was a cerebral technician in keeping with his Teutonic background. Yet his formative years in the ring were often erratic and he suffered a major defeat early on at the fists of Canadian Larry Gaines.

Max won the European heavyweight title when he KO'd the reigning champ, Michael Bonaglia in a decisive first-round encounter. The win enabled him to travel to the USA to continue his career and have a crack at the world title. He beat a number of tough opponents including 'Cleveland Rubber Man' Johnny Risko and Basque hard man Paulino Uzcudun, but returned home to Germany when no title match could be arranged.

On 13 June 1930, he returned to the States to do battle with Jack Sharkey for the coveted trophy at the Yankee Stadium, where 80,000 fans paid some $700,000 to watch the pair slug it out. Max was controversially awarded the match after the fourth round when Sharkey floored him with a low blow. Max's manager told him to stay on the canvas and hold his groin, and the ref duly awarded him the contest and the world title. The Americans, upset that the title should go overseas and in somewhat dubious circumstances, demanded a quick rematch and, after Schmeling had whipped the 'pride of Georgia', Young Stribling, in the 15th, he lost his crown to Sharkey in a 1932 rematch.

Schmeling still proved he was one of the best, beating Mickey Walker and, more astonishingly, the seemingly invincible Joe Louis. When the two met, he floored his opponent in the fourth before finishing the job in the 12th with a right-cross. Unfortunately he then returned to his homeland at the time when Germany was in the first grip of National Socialism.

Another bout with Louis was scheduled, but when the German returned to New York, the media saw him as the personification of Nazi evil. The 'Brown Bomber' wreaked his revenge,

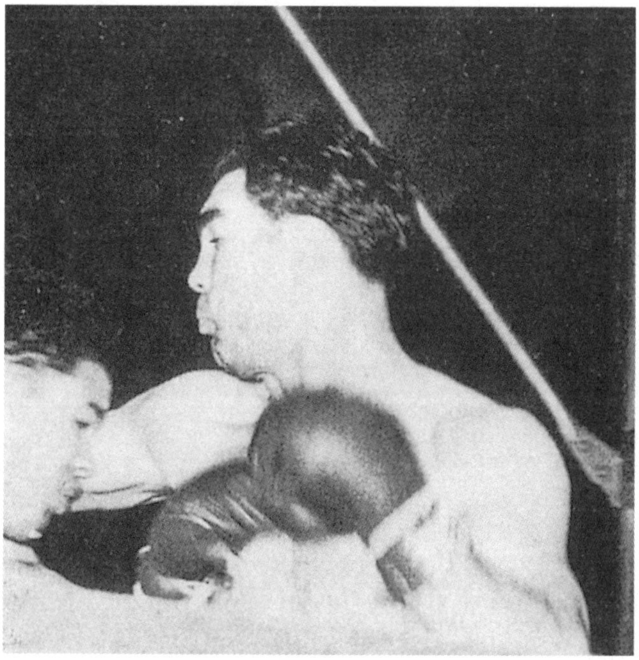

finishing the fight in just one round by flooring Max three times and breaking bones in his back with some vicious punching.

Schmeling's career was all but over. Something of a fallen hero in the eyes of the Nazi rulers, he joined up as a paratrooper as World War II began and later, after escaping from the British in Crete he was given a desk job in which, it was later discovered, he helped hundreds of Jews escape the death camps.

After the war, he gave up boxing to become a successful businessman and later sent his old opponent Joe Louis a generous donation when the latter fell on hard times.

For a man who won 56 of his 70 bouts (38 by KO), Max Schmeling will always be remembered for his cool approach and, more importantly, his sporting attitude.

Jack Sharkey

NATIONALITY	WEIGHT(S) FOUGHT	NO. OF FIGHTS	WON–LOST (KO's)	HONOURS
American	Heavyweight	55	38-13 -4 (14)	World heavy-weight cham-pion 1932-33

A Lithuanian-American, Jack Sharkey went down in boxing history as the man who was KO'd by two of the immortals — Joe Louis and Jack Dempsey.

Sharkey discovered his talent for pugilism when he joined the US Navy during World War I and became famous for his left jab when he embarked on a professional career in peacetime. He changed his Lithuanian name of Josef Paul Cukoschay to the more regular American Jack Sharkey by stealing the Christian name of another fighter he really admired, Jack Dempsey, and the surname of an equally admired turn-of-the-century boxer, Sailor Tom Sharkey. Despite an early setback when he was KO'd by Romero Rojas, Sharkey was soon racking up a series of victories including a decisive one against Irish-Bostonian Jim Maloney.

He then met hard-nut Harry Wills, also known as the 'Black Menace', and gave the ageing fighter a veritable thrashing. This victory enabled him to meet his hero, Jack Dempsey, who'd recently lost the world heavyweight title to Gene Tunney in 1926. It was a well-matched non-title contest and it looked at first as if Sharkey would get the better of the former champ and by the seventh, he was well ahead on points. But Dempsey saw his chance and KO'd Sharkey with a sharp left-hook.

The defeat did little to deter the apparently confident Sharkey and he eventually met the Australian Tom Heeney to decide who would face reigning champ 'Gentleman' Gene Tunney. The match was deemed a draw and it was the Aussie who got first crack at Tunney who severely beat him and retired on the proceeds! Sharkey carried on in what was becoming a very uneven career, losing to Johnny Risko on points but KO'ing well-respected light-heavyweight Tommy Loughran with a superb right. Eventually a world heavyweight title fight was arranged, but German Max Schmeling was awarded the title after Sharkey had punched low in the fourth.

Once described as 'always the bridesmaid but never the bride', Sharkey continued his ups and downs in the ring, flooring the giant Primo Carnera and then despatching light-heavyweight supremo, Jack Delaney. Finally, though past his prime, Sharkey got another crack at the world title, again with Max Schmeling as his opponent, in 1932 — and, though the German dominated the second half, Jack's early lead gave him the points he needed.

Ironically in his first defence of the title, he was iced by Primo Carnera whom he'd earlier so soundly KO'd! Thoroughly humiliated by this defeat, Sharkey lost that famous confidence and was subsequently trounced by the likes of Joe Louis and Max Baer.

In old age Sharkey was bitter that he'd lost his title so decisively to Carnera and, though he was never destined to go down as one of the true greats, his record of 55 bouts, of which he won 38 (14 by KO) stands as a testament to this mercurial personality.

Tony Sibson

NATIONALITY	WEIGHT(S) FOUGHT	NO. OF FIGHTS	WON–LOST (KO'S)	HONOURS
British	Middleweight, light-heavy-weight	Detailed stats not available	Detailed stats not available	British middleweight champion 1979 European middleweight champion 1980

KNOWN as the 'fighting gypsy', Tony Sibson was born in Leicester in 1958 and genuine Romany blood was said to flow through his veins.

Reputedly a boxer who lacked self-discipline, Sibson nonetheless won his first 30 contests in his native Midlands and, the day after his 21st birthday on 10 April 1979, stole the British middleweight crown from Frankie Lucas. But he lost it again the same November to the smart and courageous Kevin Finnegan. Just over a year later in December 1980, Sibson set his sights higher, determined to win the European middleweight title from Matteo Salvemini at the Albert Hall. Having won the first six rounds, the gypsy KO'd the Italian with a mass of head punches to win the crown.

In January 1981, Sibson took on Argentinian Norberto Cabrera, who knocked him down in the first. But Sibson was soon back in the race and won the contest after ten rounds, nine of which he'd won. Arguably his most famous victory came later the same year in September when he met ex-world champion Alan Minter at Wembley. It was a brutal, mercifully short contest with Sibson showing his full potential by destroying Minter in just three rounds with bad cuts and a broken nose.

In February 1982 he met American Dwight Davison in an official world championship eliminator at the Birmingham NEC. It was a close contest but the 'Leicester Romany' outpointed the taller American. When Sibson faced Marvin Hagler for the world middleweight title in Worcester, Massachusetts, in February 1983, his notorious lack of self-discipline came into play and Sibson failed to train as thoroughly as he should have. The American took the Brit apart in a mere six rounds, an humiliating experience.

The defeat strengthened his resolve — he won all of his seven European title bouts — and hunkered down to serious training in Florida to prepare for his match against 'Irish' John Collins, a Bostonite whom he despatched in just two rounds in Atlantic City. However his next fight against Don Lee in January 1984 ended in disaster with Sibson thoroughly cut up and beaten by the eighth.

His interest in the game dipped and he took the whole of 1985 off and when he did return his two important world title contests both ended in defeat. In September 1986 he went up a division to face top WBC light-heavyweight Dennis Andries but the fight was stopped in the ninth. His final appearance in February 1988 against Olympic gold medallist Frank Tate also ended sadly when the American KO'd him in the tenth.

Tony Sibson will be remembered as one of British boxing's brightest hopes whose mercurial temperament ensured he never realised his true potential.

James 'Bonecrusher' Smith

THE giant, 6ft 4in James 'Bonecrusher' Smith first came to prominence when he fought Frank Bruno at Wembley in May 1984. He'd picked up his fearsome nickname when serving with the US Army in Germany.

Hard as it is to believe, Smith didn't put on a boxing glove until 23, having been a school basketball star in his home state of Carolina. His boxing career started in earnest after leaving the Army and finding work as a prison guard. — a job that paid insufficiently to feed and clothe his family. His lack of a professional training regime caught him out when his first pro debut against up-and-coming James Broad ended in the fourth, but Smith got himself into shape and reeled off 13 straight wins, all but four ending inside the distance.

Smith, 29, returned to Europe for his 15th fight against Bruno, whose career was progressing steadily. The match appeared to be going in his opponent's favour up to the tenth round when Big Frank walked right into a bonecrushing left hook that connected with his temple and sent him falling against the ropes. 'Bonecrusher' then rained down a flurry of punches that were enough to finish the job.

Smith's career in the US began to take off, and though his bid for the IBF title against Larry Holmes in Las Vegas in November 1984 ended in failure he wrested the WBA heavyweight title from Tim Witherspoon in New York in December 1986. His first defence against Mike Tyson the following March ended in defeat when the fighting machine outpointed him over 12 rounds. As with Bruno nearly a decade later, it seemed to spell the end of his career as a top-flight challenger.

NATIONALITY	WEIGHT(S) FOUGHT	NO. OF FIGHTS	WON–LOST (KO's)	HONOURS
American	Heavyweight	Detailed stats not available	Detailed stats not available	Detailed stats not available

Leon Spinks

LEON Spinks (born in St Louis on 11 July 1953) held the world's most prestigious title for just six months but his defeat of Muhammad Ali remains one of boxing's biggest upsets.

Spinks, whose younger brother Michael later found fame and fortune as world light-heavyweight and heavyweight champion, won the light-heavyweight gold at the 1976 Olympics but had done nothing to suggest he could trouble the legendary Ali in just his eighth professional fight. But the champion, looking overweight and undertrained, was constantly beaten to the punch by the rampant Spinks, who looked on the verge of forcing a stoppage at times and thoroughly outpointed his opponent over 15 rounds on 15 February 1978.

However, seven months later to the day on 15 September Ali, his 36-year old body marbled to the minute, outfoxed and frustrated his inexperienced but brave rival to win back the heavyweight title for an unprecedented third time. Sadly this was to prove a painful fall from grace for the unfortunate Spinks, whose indiscipline and lack of basic education left him ill-equipped for his rapid rise to fame.

Thrashed in a subsequent title eliminator by South African Gerrie Coetzee, Spinks had a third shot at the world crown in 1981 but was humiliated by Larry Holmes in three painful rounds. Spinks, who subsequently tried his hand as a cruiserweight, became a somewhat pathetic figure as he fought on unsuccessfully into the 1990s, but the hungry young fighter who shocked the 'Greatest' has his own place in history.

NATIONALITY	WEIGHT(S) FOUGHT	NO. OF FIGHTS	WON–LOST (KO's)	HONOURS
Swedish	Heavyweight	28	26-2	European heavyweight champion 1956-59, 1962-63 World champion 1959-60

Michael Spinks

MICHAEL Spinks was not only one of the best light-heavyweight champions the sport has produced, but also beat one of the best heavyweight champions of all time, Larry Holmes.

In fact, in so doing Spinks (born 13 July 1956) created two firsts; he became the first light-heavyweight title holder to win the world heavyweight championship and, following Leon, who defeated and was beaten by Muhammad Ali for the crown, they became the first brothers to hold the top weight title.

After winning a gold medal at the Montreal Olympics in 1976, Spinks turned professional and soon sped up the light-heavyweight rankings with fine victories over fighters like Ramon Ranquello and Willie Taylor. He knocked out Marvin Johnson and then captured the WBA crown with a points decision over holder Eddie Mustapha Muhammad. He knocked back his next five challengers.

In 1983 Spinks met WBC champion Dwight Braxton in a bid to unify the titles and won the fight on points to become the undisputed champion in the light-heavy division. But it was the decision to move up to heavy and his shock beating of the formerly undefeated Holmes, that made Michael Spinks a household name — and a good deal of money.

Holmes had won 48 contests and needed just one more to equal the record of the great Rocky Marciano, but the awkward Spinks scored a narrow points victory over his heavier opponent. He defended his title successfully once, knocking out Steffen Tangstad, before being stripped of his IBF crown for fighting the great white hope Gerry Cooney instead of Tony Tucker.

However, an attempt to tackle the then unbeaten Mike Tyson in 1988 ended in disaster with Iron Mike knocking Spinks out in 91 seconds of the first round. Spinks retired after his first setback with a record of 31-1, which included 21 KOs.

NATIONALITY	WEIGHT(S) FOUGHT	NO. OF FIGHTS	WON–LOST (KO's)	HONOURS
American	Light-heavyweight, heavyweight	32	31-1 (21)	WBA light-heavyweight champion 1981-83 World light-heavyweight champion 1983-85 IBF heavyweight champion 1985-87 (88)

Teofilio Stevenson

BORN in Cuba in 1952, Teofilio became the second man in history to win three Olympic gold medals — and he did it in the toughest division of all, the heavyweight. Over the years the Olympics have produced some of the all-time greats: Muhammad Ali, George Foreman and Joe Frazier all won gold medals before turning professional. Incredibly, though, Stevenson never joined the pro ranks.

He won his first gold as a 20-year old in Munich but, despite several big-money offers, Stevenson would not give up his amateur status. 'I don't like the way professional fighters are handled,' said the Cuban.

Stevenson then went on to win the world heavyweight championship before again taking the gold medal at the 1976 Montreal Games. The offers for him to turn pro grew ever more bigger, but still Teo would not be tempted. Again the talented 6ft 3in champion lifted the world heavyweight belt before competing in the Moscow Olympics. Unlike previous finals Stevenson's opponent at least managed to survive the three rounds but the Cuban still took the gold.

Teofilio Stevenson, the three-time Olympic champion may well be able to stake a claim on being one of the greatest boxers ever, if not the greatest. But he never fought as a professional. Ali, Foreman, Frazier, Leon Spinks, Ken Norton, Larry Holmes, John Tate and Mike Weaver were all world heavyweight champions during Stevenson's Olympic reign. How Teofilio Stevenson would have fared against them we'll never know . . .

NATIONALITY	WEIGHT(S) FOUGHT	NO. OF FIGHTS	WON–LOST (KO's)	HONOURS
				As he is an amateur, figures are not available

John H. Stracey

EAST Londoner John Henry Stracey (born 22 September 1950) sparked a mass of early Christmas parties in his native Bethnal Green when, in December 1975, he ended the career of the great Cuban Jose Napoles to lift the WBC welterweight title in Mexico City.

Stracey, the British and European champion and another from the winning stable of Terry Lawless, was given little chance of success even though Napoles, who had successfully defended his laurels 13 times, was well into his 36th year. But the East Ender answered his critics by climbing off the floor in the opening round to sensationally stop his opponent in six rounds.

An accurate puncher whose 37 career knockouts came from an accumulation of punches rather than one telling blow, Stracey overpowered American Hedgemon Lewis in 10 rounds in March the following year, but despite stating his need for a rest was pushed into another defence three months later against the strong-punching Mexican Carlos Palomino. The challenger, who went on to successfully defend his title seven times, ended Stracey's short reign when another of his numerous attacks to the body paid dividends in the 12th.

Stracey fought on but ran into another eager young British fighter named Dave 'Boy' Green — another world title victim of Palomino — who beat him in 10 rounds in 1977. Stracey, who represented his country at lightweight in the 1968 Olympics and lifted the ABA light-welterweight title a year later in his amateur days, quit the sport the following year.

NATIONALITY	WEIGHT(S) FOUGHT	NO. OF FIGHTS	WON–LOST (KO's)	HONOURS
British	Welterweight	51	45-5-1 (37)	British welterweight champion 1973 European welterweight champion 1974 WBC welterweight champion 1975-76

John L. Sullivan

ALTHOUGH more than 100 years have elapsed since he lost the world heavyweight championship, John L. Sullivan remains a legendary figure in the sport of boxing.

Sullivan was born in Roxbury on 15 October 1858, Massachusetts and starting to gain attention at the age of 19. Although he was only 5ft 10in tall he was immensely strong and weighed nearly 200lb.

He won the world championship in 1882 in Mississippi City when, in a bare knuckles fight, he knocked out Paddy Ryan in the ninth round to begin a 10-year reign as heavyweight king. Sullivan then began a tour of the United States offering money to anyone who would take him on and beat him but, despite all comers, he repelled all challenges.

He always loved a drink, but had the amazing ability to recover from his heavy drinking sessions in time to get his body back in shape, even though the training sessions would have killed a horse!

After drawing with Charley Mitchell over 39 rounds in France in 1888, Sullivan fought the last bare-knuckle heavyweight title bout against the formidable Jake Kilrain in Mississippi a year later. Amazingly, despite fighting in over 100-degree heat, Sullivan held on to his title when Kilrain quit after the 75th round.

But time ran out for the big man when, in 1892, Sullivan met the stylish James J. Corbett at New Orleans. In the first heavyweight title bout to be fought under the Marquis of Queensberry Rules, Corbett outboxed and then knocked him out in 21 rounds.

The result shocked the nation and Sullivan never again fought and retired honourably with a record of 38-3-1, including 33 knockouts. In later life Sullivan stopped drinking and even toured the country lecturing on the evils of alcohol.

NATIONALITY	WEIGHT(S) FOUGHT	NO. OF FIGHTS	WON–LOST (KO's)	HONOURS
American	Heavyweight	42	38-1-3(33)	World champion champion 1882-92

Ernie Terrell

STANDING a gigantic 6ft 6in tall, Ernie Terrell was born in Chicago, Illinois on 4 April 1939 and will be remembered for his famous bout with Muhammad Ali. He turned professional in 1958, but his early career showed no signs of greatness. It was in 1963 that he first began to be noticed with victories over Cleveland Williams and Zora Folley.

When the WBA stripped reigning champ Cassius Clay of his world heavyweight status for his deep-seated religious and political views in early 1965, the title was vacant — and, in March, Terrell beat Eddie Machen for the crown on points. Terrell retained the title against Canadian George Chuvalo in the November and again against Doug Jones in Houston, Texas in June 1966, outpointing both opponents.

Finally reinstated by the WBA, Clay, now known by his Black Muslim name of Muhammad Ali, was paired with Terrell in Houston on 6 February 1967. By this time Ernie had remained unbeaten for five years. Throughout the match he baited Ali, calling him by his previous name of Clay, to which Ali riposted with 'Uncle Tom'. Ali took control almost straight away, constantly landing punches on the champ and demanding 'What's my name?' with each blow. Terrell suffered a badly cut eye and was easily outpointed over 15 rounds as Ali put on a show of both dazzling skill and unremitting cruelty which was enough to force his humiliated opponent into retirement.

Though he made one poor attempt at a comeback, Terrell gave up the ring leaving behind a solid enough record of 55 bouts, 46 wins and 9 defeats.

NATIONALITY	WEIGHT(S) FOUGHT	NO. OF FIGHTS	WON–LOST (KO's)	HONOURS
American	Heavyweight	55	46-9	WBA heavyweight champion 1965-67

Pinklon Thomas

Felix Trinidad

THOMAS shot to fame in 1984 when he challenged fellow American Tim Witherspoon to the WBC heavyweight title in Las Vegas on 31 August. It was Witherspoon's first defence of the crown, but Thomas outpointed the reigning champ in 12 rounds.

Thomas successfully defended his newly won title against Mike Weaver on 15 June the following year by KO'ing the contender in the eighth. However, Trevor Berbick stole the title from him on 22 March 1986 on points, again in Las Vegas.

The crown was being exchanged at an alarming rate — Berbick duly lost it to Mike Tyson, which gave Thomas the chance for another crack at the reigning champ on 30 May 1987. The ref, however, stopped the bout in Tyson's favour in the sixth round.

Thomas carried on fighting, his bouts including a defeat at the hands of champ-to-be Riddick Bowe, but he looked unlikely to get near to the top of the ladder again, and publicly admitted that he'd been fighting a severe drug addiction.

NATIONALITY	WEIGHT(S) FOUGHT	NO. OF FIGHTS	WON–LOST (KO's)	HONOURS
American	Heavyweight	Detailed stats not available	Detailed stats not available	WBC heavyweight champion 1984-86

BORN on 10 January 1973 in Cupey Alto, Puerto Rico, Felix Trinidad has risen from humble beginnings to become IBF welterweight champion. The boxing world was made aware of the potential of the man in only his first fight in 1990 when Trinidad stopped Angel Romero inside two rounds. He won his next 18 contests with some considerable ease, only two of them — against Darren McGrew and Jake Rodriguez — going the distance.

His dream of winning a world title became a reality three years after his debut. On paper, Felix was up against his toughest opponent to date in the shape of Maurice Blocker. But the IBF welterweight championship of the world was on its way back to Puerto Rico as early as the second round.

To date he has defended the title on 12 occasions. This impressive record has included comprehensive victories against the likes of Rodney Moore, Fred Pendleton, Ray Lovato and Kevin Lueshing. Only once has he been taken the full 12 rounds. This was against a formidable opponent in the shape of Hector Camacho, but it was Trinidad who took the decision on points.

He's not up there with the all-time greats at the moment but Felix Trinidad may yet go on to earn that distinction.

NATIONALITY	WEIGHT(S) FOUGHT	NO. OF FIGHTS	WON–LOST (KO's)	HONOURS
Puerto Rico	Welterweight	30	30-0 (26)	IBF welterweight champion 1993-

Gene Tunney

NEW York-born Gene Tunney (born 25 May 1897) boasts a record to be proud of but the heavyweight champion of the world between 1926-28 is now best remembered for the 'long-count' controversy in his second fight with Jack Dempsey.

Tunney, who always nurtured ambitions to be a world champion fighter despite his impressive academic achievements, had comfortably beaten the Manassa Mauler in their first fight in September 1926, ending Dempsey's seven-year reign. But, floored in the seventh round of their rematch a year later, Tunney was down for 14 seconds after Dempsey failed to retreat to a neutral corner. Recovering well, the ex-Marine retained his title with a 10-round points decision.

Tunney retired a wealthy man after just one more defence, when he beat Tom Heeney of New Zealand on an 11th-round stoppage. He became a successful businessman and the father of a US Senator before his death in November 1978.

Gene Tunney's record bears the fiercest scrutiny. Starting as a light-heavyweight, he stormed through his first 14 fights before joining the Marines, where he won the US Expeditionary Force championship. Back in Civvy Street, he continued where he left off to win the American light-heavyweight title, only to lose it after a fearful battering from Harry Greb.

Forced to re-evaluate his style, he was never beaten again, vanquishing Greb four times in subsequent matches before moving up to take on the heavyweights. His career total of 62 wins, 19 no decisions, one no contest and just one defeat is highly impressive.

NATIONALITY	WEIGHT(S) FOUGHT	NO. OF FIGHTS	WON–LOST (KO's)	HONOURS
American	Light-heavy-weight, heavy-weight	77	57-1-19 (42)	American light-heavy-weight champion 1922, 1923 World heavy-weight champion 1926-28

Randolph Turpin

NATIONALITY	WEIGHT(S) FOUGHT	NO. OF FIGHTS	WON–LOST (KO's)	HONOURS
British	Middleweight, light-heavyweight	73	64-8-1	British middleweight champion 1950-54 European middleweight champion 1951-54 World middleweight champion 1951 Empire middleweight champion 1952-54 British light-heavyweight champion 1952, 1955 Empire light-heavyweight champion 1952-55

BORN in 1928 to a Jamaican father and white mother, Randolph Turpin had to endure emotional and physical hardship in addition to all the attendant racism of the era, but still went on to become one of the true heroes of British boxing.

Having suffered severe illness as a baby, Turpin's health was further damaged as a 12-year old when he lost his hearing in one ear after nearly drowning. His father died when he was still a youngster but he was bestowed with an awesome talent — the ability to deal a one-blow knockout. He won the ABA junior and senior titles when still a 17-year old.

The first setback of his career came during his 20th professional match in 1950 against Albert Finch, though Turpin stopped the more experienced fighter in the fifth round of a return match later the same year to win the British middleweight crown. In 1951 he won the European title with a one-punch KO of Dutchman Luc Van Dam.

But his real '15 minutes of fame' came on 10 July 1951 when his 44th professional contest matched him against one of the giants of boxing, Sugar Ray Robinson, at Earl's Court. It was the seventh fight for the US champ on a six-week European tour and he was feeling on top of the world, having easily seen off all his opponents. But right from the start the pugnacious Brit dominated the match and by the seventh round the American was suffering a badly cut left eye. He was unable to penetrate Turpin's superior strength and the Brit successfully outpointed the legend over the full 15 rounds.

His moment of glory was shortlived — barely nine weeks later, Turpin had to again defend his world title against the man he'd so recently beaten and this time Robinson had the full measure of his opponent. It was a fairly even contest but, after a head-on collision cut his eye badly in the tenth round, Robinson drew on all his reserves to pin Turpin to the ropes and land a winning volley of blows.

It was the turning point in Turpin's career - his personal life began to be plagued by domestic and money troubles, though he won the British light-heavyweight title from Don Cockell and, losing weight, again made the Empire and European middleweight titles his own. It looked like he might again wrest back the world middleweight title, this time from Carl 'BoBo' Olsen, but the Swedish-American outboxed him on points.

He carried on boxing but never regained the momentum of his early career — he managed to see off three challenges to his British title before Yolande Pompey dethroned him in September 1958 after just two rounds. His business dealings failed and after a period as a professional wrestler, with the tax people closing in, he committed suicide in 1966 aged 37. It was a sad end for this giant of British boxing.

Mike Tyson

BOXING had been looking for almost a decade for a heavyweight champion to fill the void left by the demise of Muhammad Ali. On 22 November 1986 it found him when Mike Tyson (born 30 June 1966) battered Trevor Berbick to defeat in two rounds to lift the WBC crown and become the youngest ever heavyweight champion.

At just 20 years and 145 days, the fearsome Tyson had exploded to the top. From his first pro fight in March 1985, when he stopped Hector Mercedes in one round, he had despatched 27 opponents, the first 19 in 37 rounds. Probably shorter than his official 5ft 11in, Tyson's stalking manner, fast hands and incredible strength gave him a terrifying ring presence which successfully intimidated his opponents.

Wins over 'Bonecrusher' Smith, Tyrell Biggs, Larry Holmes, Michael Spinks, Frank Bruno and Carl Williams, the last five all stopped, cemented Tyson as the world's undisputed champion by 1989 but, amid scandal in his private life and rumours he was refusing to train, the boy from the ghetto was sensationally knocked out by 'Buster' Douglas in Tokyo. Several well-publicised dramas, including a divorce, street brawl and finally a rape charge, ended with Tyson jailed for three years.

On his release, Tyson won a couple of warm-up fights before regaining the WBC title from Britain's Frank Bruno and the WBA version from the equally-petrified Bruce Seldon. His air of invincibility apparently back, Tyson defended against former champion Evander Holyfield and in one of the most memorable fights in living memory, Holyfield proved Tyson mortal by stopping him after 11 magnificent rounds. Their rematch, the richest prize fight ever arranged, is eagerly awaited.

NATIONALITY	WEIGHT(S) FOUGHT	NO. OF FIGHTS	WON–LOST (KO's)	HONOURS
American	Heavyweight	47	45-2 (39)	WBC heavyweight champion 1986-90 WBA heavyweight champion 1987-90 IBF heavyweight champion 1989-90 WBC heavyweight champion 1996 WBA heavyweight champion 1996

Jersey Joe Walcott

BORN Arnold Raymond Cream in New Jersey on 31 January 1914, Jersey Joe Walcott made fight history in July 1951 when, aged 37, he knocked out Ezzard Charles to become the oldest man to win the world heavyweight championship.

Walcott was winning the title at the fifth attempt, having in 1947 been grudgingly offered a shot at Joe Louis's belt by the New York Commission, who questioned the 33-year old's right to be in the same ring as the great man. As it turned out, Walcott twice had the champion on the floor before losing a split decision. Given a rematch, Walcott was knocked out in 11 rounds.

Two more challenges followed in 1949 and 1951, both against Ezzard Charles, who twice outscored him over 15 rounds. But, four months after the second defeat, Walcott climbed in with Charles again and, despite being the complete underdog, fought superbly before a right cross-shot and powerhouse left-hook took out the champion in the seventh round.

In the fourth meeting between the two 11 months later, Walcott defied his 38 years to win on points. But in September of the same year, despite putting up a spirited defence, he lost the title to an up-and-coming 'Rocky' Marciano. Walcott had the challenger on the canvas in the first round and had built up a big points lead going into the last third of the fight. However, Marciano's strength began to tell and a KO in the 13th spared his opponent any further punishment. Given a return in May 1953, Walcott was humbled in one round and retired.

NATIONALITY	WEIGHT(S) FOUGHT	NO. OF FIGHTS	WON–LOST (KO's)	HONOURS
Barbadian/American	Welterweight	68	50-17-1 (30)	World welterweight champion 1897-98, 1901-06

Jim Watt

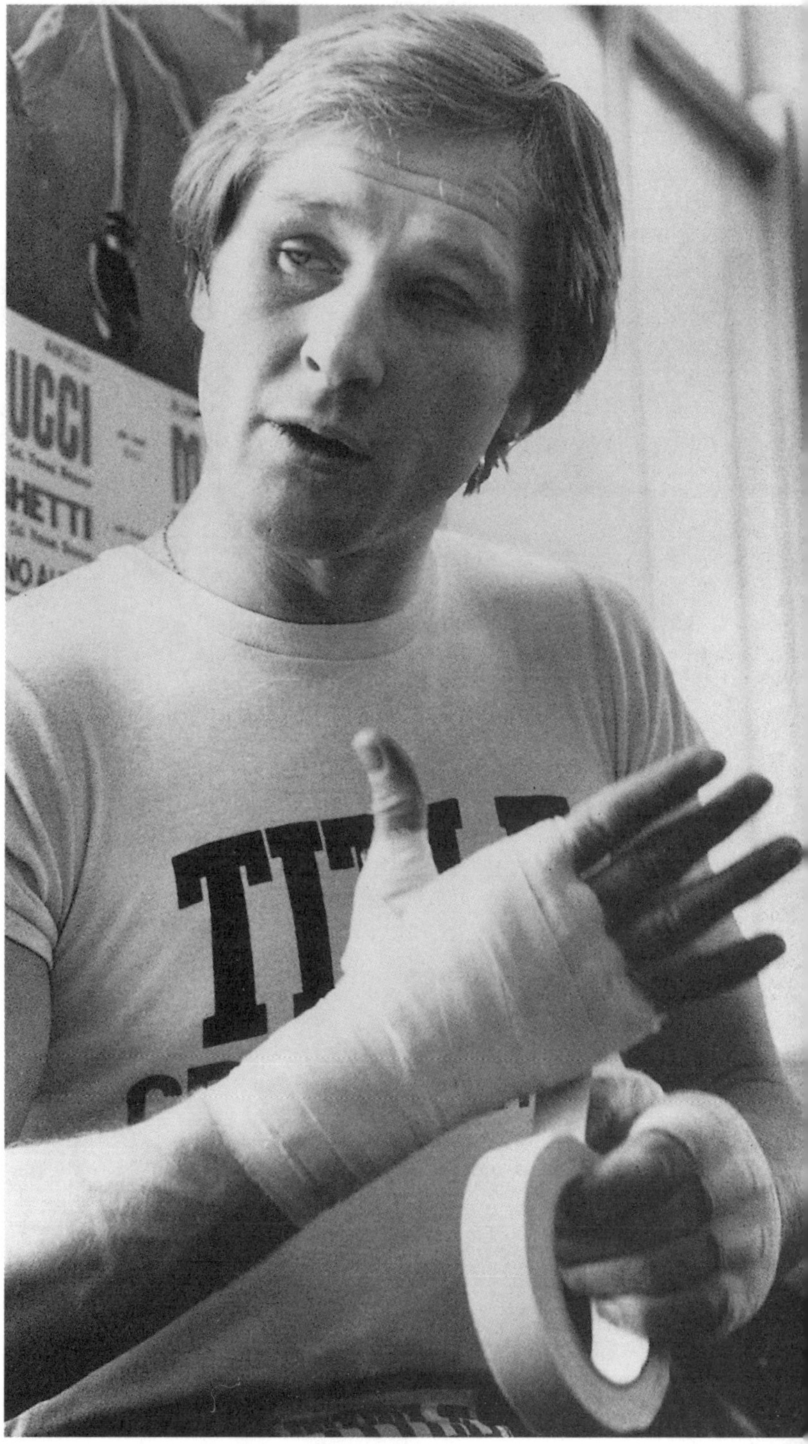

BRITAIN has produced better world champions than Jim Watt, born in Glasgow on 18 July 1948, but few more dedicated to his art. His two-year reign at the top was richly deserved and highly cherished after 11 years as a professional.

Watt's early career took time to gather momentum. An ABA title winner, he had just 14 fights (one defeat) in four years after joining the paid ranks in 1968. He finally challenged Willie Reilly for the British lightweight crown in 1972, only to lose in 10 rounds. After winning the crown vacated by Reilly, Watt lost it to his better-known fellow countryman Ken Buchanan, the former world title holder beaten the year before by the legendary Roberto Duran.

Watt regained the British title in 1977 when Buchanan relinquished it, and stepped out of his shadow forever on 17 April 1979 when his persistent onslaught stopped Colombia's Alfredo Pituala after 12 rounds for the vacant WBC world title. Watt's painstaking, points-building style and relentless pressure saw him tot up four successful defences, three inside the distance and a points verdict over previously unbeaten American Howard Davis, an Olympic Games gold medallist.

His run was brought to an end in June 1981 by the brilliant Nicaraguan Alexis Arguello, but only after 15 gruelling rounds, every one bitterly contested by the proud Scot. He retired with 38 wins (38 KOs) from 46 contests, a vastly underrated world champion with an enormous will to win. He became an accomplished fight analyser for television and currently works for Sky TV.

NATIONALITY	WEIGHT(S) FOUGHT	NO. OF FIGHTS	WON–LOST (KO's)	HONOURS
British	Lightweight	46	38-8 (28)	British lightweight champion 1973-4, 1977-78 WBC lightweight champion 1979-81

Pernell Whitaker

BORN in Norfolk, Virginia, on 2 January 1964 Whitaker, with a fight record of 39-1-1 (15 KOs), first became known when winning the Olympic lightweight gold medal in 1984. He turned pro and took the NABF title with a 12-round decision over Roger Mayweather, but lost his next bout to Jose Luis Ramirez in controversial fashion. Despite breaking his left hand it seemed he had done enough to win but the points verdict went to Ramirez — a decision condemned as one of the worst in boxing history.

Whitaker bounced back to defeat IBF lightweight champion Greg Haugen before avenging his loss against Ramirez, taking his WBC crown in the process. In 1990 Whitaker defended his IBF and WBC titles with victories over Freddie Pendleton and Azumah Nelson. He then knocked out WBA champion Juan Nazario to become the first undisputed world lightweight champion since Roberto Duran, a decade before.

In 1992 Pernell moved up to junior-welterweight and won the IBF title against Rafael Pineda before taking the WBC welterweight crown from Buddy McGirt. Whitaker then claimed the WBA junior-middleweight with a convincing win over Julio Cesar Chavez. That meant the southpaw boxer had gone from Olympic gold to four world titles. It is no surprise that many say Pernell Whitaker is the best pound-for-pound fighter in the sport.

NATIONALITY	WEIGHT(S) FOUGHT	NO. OF FIGHTS	WON–LOST (KO'S)	HONOURS
American	Lightweight, light-welterweight, welterweight, light-middleweight	41	39-1-1 (16)	IBF lightweight champion 1989-92 WBC lightweight champion 1989-92 WBA lightweight champion 1989-92 IBF light-welterweight champion 1992-93 WBC welterweight champion 1993-97 WBA light-middleweight champion 1995

Jess Willard

JESS Willard is best remembered for ending the career of one great heavyweight champion and starting another's than for winning the title itself.

A wheat farmer in Kansas, Willard (born 29 December 1881) — at a comparatively advanced age — entered professional boxing in the era of the 'White Hope', when promoters were seeking white contenders for the title held by the great Jack Johnson, a black who was the focus of much racial animosity.

Willard is still one of the biggest heavyweight champs, standing 6ft 5in and weighing around 250lb. After attaining worthy draws with Luther McCarty and Arthur Pelkey and losing to Gunboat Smith, Willard produced a hot streak of victories from 11 contests to earn a title tilt at Johnson.

Johnson, the first black heavyweight champion after beating Tommy Burns, was forced to flee the United States after a trumped-up charge under the Mann Act was levelled at him. After defending his title several times overseas, including in England, Johnson was eventually persuaded to give the challenger his chance in 1915 in Cuba. Willard knocked Johnson out in 26 rounds, although the loser was later to claim he threw the fight in order to re-establish himself back in the States.

The 'Pottawatomie Giant', as Willard was called after the area he farmed in, was not an active champion, making only one defence — against Frank Moran — before tackling Jack Dempsey four years later. But, aged 37 and not well trained, Willard was no match for the hungry and destructive Dempsey, who despatched him in three rounds after putting him down seven times in the first.

Willard briefly returned to the ring four years later, but after losing to Luis Angel Firpo in eight rounds he bowed out with a record that read 24-6-1, including 21 knockouts.

NATIONALITY	WEIGHT(S) FOUGHT	NO. OF FIGHTS	WON–LOST (KO's)	HONOURS
American		35	23-6-6(20)	World heavyweight champion 1915-19

Tim Witherspoon

BORN in Pontiac, Michigan, on 27 December 1957, Witherspoon started boxing when his folks moved to Philadelphia. He turned pro in 1979, having won six out of his seven amateur bouts, and proved a good all-round technician with a savage right hand that could come over the top of an unwary opponent's defences.

Having tackled tough opposition like Alfonzo Ratliff and Renaldo Snipes, Witherspoon had his first crack at the WBC title in Las Vegas on 20 May 1983 against reigning champ Larry Holmes, who'd already successfully defended his crown 14 times. Tim didn't upset the applecart, with Holmes outpointing him in 12 rounds, though the decision was disputed.

When Holmes gave up his crown to fight for the IBF, Witherspoon fought Greg Page for the vacant title and won it on points in 12 rounds on 9 March 1984. He lost it in his first defence to Pinklon Thomas the following August, but still hadn't taken a count in either his amateur or professional careers.

Despite the setback, Witherspoon wrested back the title on 17 January 1986, outpointing Tony Tubbs in Atlanta, Georgia, and made a thrilling defence against Frank Bruno at Wembley in July in what was his 27th professional fight (25 wins). His second reign proved a short one, however, when 'Bonecrusher' Smith spectacularly KO'd him in the opening round on 12 December 1986 in New York.

No more championships have come the way of 'Terrible Tim' — the nickname he gained when a young sparring partner for Muhammad Ali — though bouts with the likes of Mike Tyson followed.

NATIONALITY	WEIGHT(S) FOUGHT	NO. OF FIGHTS	WON–LOST (KO's)	HONOURS
American	Heavyweight	47	43-4	WBC heavyweight champion 1984 WBA heavyweight champion 1986

OVERLEAF: 'Duke' McKenzie fights de Luca in March 1989.

Heavyweight

	WBC	WBA	IBF	WBO
1978	Larry Holmes (2)	Muhammad Ali (1)	—	—
1979	Larry Holmes (3)	John Tate (1)	—	—
1980	Larry Holmes (4)	Mike Weaver (2)	—	—
1981	Larry Holmes (3)	Mike Weaver (1)	—	—
1982	Larry Holmes (2)	Mike Dokes (1)	—	—
1983	Larry Holmes (3)	Mike Dokes (1)/ Gerrie Coetzee (1)	—	—
1984	Tim Witherspoon (1)/ Pinklon Thomas (1)	Greg Page (1)	Larry Holmes (1)	—
1985	Pinklon Thomas (1)	Tony Tubbs (1)	Larry Holmes (2)/ Mike Spinks (1)	—
1986	Trevor Berbick (1)/ Mike Tyson (1)	Tim Witherspoon (2)/ James 'Bonecrusher' Smith (1)	Mike Spinks (2)	—
1987	Mike Tyson (4)	Mike Tyson (4)	Tony Tucker (1)/ Mike Tyson (2)	—
1988	Mike Tyson (3)	Mike Tyson (3)	Mike Tyson (3)	—
1989	Mike Tyson (2)	Mike Tyson (2)	Mike Tyson (2)	Francesco Damiani (2)
1990	James 'Buster' Douglas (1)/ Evander Holyfield (1)	James 'Buster' Douglas (1)/ Evander Holyfield (1)	James 'Buster' Douglas (1)/ Evander Holyfield (1)	Francesco Damiani (0)
1991	Evander Holyfield (2)	Evander Holyfield (2)	Evander Holyfield (2)	Ray Mercer (2)
1992	Evander Holyfield (1)/ Riddick Bowe (1)	Evander Holyfield (1)/ Riddick Bowe (1)	Evander Holyfield (1)/ Riddick Bowe (1)	Michael Moorer (1)
1993	Lennox Lewis (2)	Riddick Bowe (2)/ Evander Holyfield (1)	Riddick Bowe (2)/ Evander Holyfield (1)	Tommy Morrison (1)/ Michael Bentt (1)
1994	Lennox Lewis (1)/ Oliver McCall (1)	Michael Moorer (1)/ George Foreman (1)	Michael Moorer (1)/ George Foreman (1)	Herbie Hide (1)
1995	Oliver McCall (1)/ Frank Bruno (1)	Bruce Seldon (2)	George Foreman (1)/ Frans Botha (1)	Riddick Bowe (2)
1996	Mike Tyson (1)	Mike Tyson (1)/ Evander Holyfield (1)	Michael Moorer (2)	Henry Akinwande (?+2)
1997	Lennox Lewis (1)		Michael Moorer (1)	Henry Akinwande (1)

Cruiserweight

	WBC	WBA	IBF	WBO
1980	Marvin Camel (1)/ Carlos DeLeon (1)	—	—	—
1981	Carlos DeLeon (0)	—	—	—
1982	Carlos DeLeon (1)/ ST Gordon (1)	Ossie Ocasio (2)	—	—
1983	ST Gordon (1)/ Carlos DeLeon (2)	Ossie Ocasio (1)	Marvin Camel (2)	—
1984	Carlos DeLeon (2)	Ossie Ocasio (1)/ Piet Crous (1)	Lee Roy Murphy (2)	—
1985	Alfonso Ratliff (1)/ Bernard Benton (1)	Piet Crous (1)/ Dwight Muhammad Qawi (1)	Lee Roy Murphy (1)	—
1986	Carlos DeLeon (2)	Dwight Muhammad Qawi (1)/ Evander Holyfield (1)	Lee Roy Murphy (1)/ Rickey Parkey (1)	—
1987	Carlos DeLeon (1)	Evander Holyfield (3)	Evander Holyfield (3)	—
1988	Carlos De Leon (1)/ Evander Holyfield (2)	Evander Holyfield (1)	Evander Holyfield (1)	—
1989	Carlos DeLeon (1)	Taoufik Belbouli (1)/ Robert Daniels (1)	Glenn McCrory (2)	Boone Pultz (1)
1990	Carlos DeLeon (1)/ Masimiliano Duran (2)	Robert Daniels (2)	Jeff Lampkin (2)	Magne Havnaa (2)
1991	Anaclet Wamba (2)	Bobby Czyz (2)	James Warring (2)	Magne Havnaa (1)
1992	Anaclet Wamba (2)	Bobby Czyz (1)	James Warring (1)/ Al Cole (1)	Tyrone Booze (2)
1993	Anaclet Wamba (2)	Orlin Norris (1)	Al Cole (3)	Marcus Bott (1)/ Nestor Giovannini (2)
1994	Anaclet Wamba (2)	Orlin Norris (3)	Al Cole (1)	Nestor Giovannini (1)/ Dariusz Michalczewski (1)
1995	Marcelo Dominguez (3)	Orlin Norris (1)/ Nate Miller (1)	Al Cole (1)	Ralf Rocchigiani (3)
1996	Marcelo Dominguez (2)	Nate Miller (3)	Adolpho Washington (1)	Ralf Rocchigiani (? + 2)
1997		Nate Miller (1)		Ralf Rocchigiani (1)

Light-Heavyweight

	WBC	WBA	IBF	WBO
1978	Mate Parlov (2)/ Marvin Johnson (1)	Victor Galindez (1)/ Mike Rossman (2)	—	—
1979	Matthew Saad Muhammad (2)	Victor Galindez (1)/ Marvin Johnson (1)	—	—
1980	Matthew Saad Muhammad (4)	Eddie Mustafa Muhammad (3)	—	—
1981	Matthew Saad Muhammad (3)/ Dwight Braxton (1)	Michael Spinks (2)	—	—
1982	Dwight Braxton (3)	Michael Spinks (4)	—	—
1983	Michael Spinks (2)	Michael Spinks (2)	—	—
1984	Michael Spinks (1)	Michael Spinks (1)	—	—
1985	Michael Spinks (2)/ JB Williamson (1)	Michael Spinks (2)	Slobodan Kacar (1)	—
1986	Dennis Andries (2)	Marvin Johnson (2)	Bobby Czyz (2)	—
1987	Thomas Hearns (1)/ Donny Lalonde (1)	Leslie Stewart (1)/ Virgil Hill (2)	Bobby Czyz (2)/ Prince Charles Williams (1)	—
1988	Donny Lalonde (1)/ Sugar Ray Leonard (1)	Virgil Hill (3)	Prince Charles Williams (2)	Michael Moorer (1)
1989	Dennis Andries (1)/ Jeff Harding (2)	Virgil Hill (3)	Prince Charles Williams (1)	Michael Moorer (6)
1990	Jeff Harding (1)/ Dennis Andries (2)	Virgil Hill (2)	Prince Charles Williams (1)	Michael Moorer (3)
1991	Dennis Andries (1)/ Jeff Harding (1)	Virgil Hill (1)/ Thomas Hearns (1)	Prince Charles Williams (4)	Leeonzer Barber (1)
1992	Jeff Harding (2)	Iran Barkley (1)/ Virgil Hill (1)	Prince Charles Williams (0)	Leeonzer Barber (1)
1993	Jeff Harding (0)	Virgil Hill (3)	Henry Maske (2)	Leeonzer Barber (2)
1994	Mike McCallum (1)	Virgil Hill (1)	Henry Maske (3)	Leeonzer Barber (1)/ Dariusz Michalczewski (1)
1995	Mike McCallum (1)/ Fabrice Tiozzo (1)	Virgil Hill (2)	Henry Maske (3)	Dariusz Michalczewski (4)
1996	Fabrice Tiozzo (1)/ Roy Jones (1)	Virgil Hill (2)	Henry Maske (2)/ Virgil Hill (1)	Dariusz Michalczewski (? + 3)
1997	Montell Griffin (1)			

Super-Middleweight

	WBC	WBA	IBF	WBO
1984	—	—	Murray Sutherland (1)/ Chong-Pai Park (1)	—
1985	—	—	Chong-Pai Park (2)	—
1986	—	—	Chong-Pai Park (3)	—
1987	—	Chong-Pai Park (1)	Chong-Pai Park (3)	—
1988	Sugar Ray Leonard (1)	Chong-Pai Park (1)/ Fulgencio Obelmejias (1)	Graciano Rocchigiani (3)	Thomas Hearns (1)
1989	Sugar Ray Leonard (2)	Inchul Baek (2)	Graciano Rocchigiani (1)	Thomas Hearns (0)
1990	Mauro Galvano (1)	Inchul Baek (1)/ Christophe Tiozzo (3)	Lindell Holmes (3)	Thomas Hearns (1)
1991	Mauro Galvano (1)	Victor Cordoba (2)	Lindell Holmes (1)/ Darrin Van Horn (2)	Chris Eubank (1)
1992	Mauro Galvano (1)/ Nigel Benn (1)	Michael Nunn (1)	Iran Barkley (1)	Chris Eubank (5)
1993	Nigel Benn (3)	Michael Nunn (4)	James Toney (2)	Chris Eubank (3)
1994	Nigel Benn (2)	Steve Little (1)/ Frank Liles (2)	James Toney (2)/ Roy Jones (1)	Chris Eubank (6)
1995	Nigel Benn (3)	Frank Liles (2)	Roy Jones (3)	Steve Collins (3)
1996	Sugarboy Malinga (1)/ Vincenzo Nardiello (1)/ Robin Reid (1)	Frank Liles (1)	Roy Jones (2)	Steve Collins (? + 2)
1997	Robin Reid (1)	Frank Liles (1)		Steve Collins (1)

ABOVE: Max Schmeling fighting Harry Thomas at Madison Square Garden, New York, December 1937. In 1934 Schmeling became the only fighter to win the heavyweight title on a disqualification.

LEFT: Henry Armstrong (left) versus Ernie Roderick, May 1939. Armstrong was the holder of three championships at different weights in 1938.

RIGHT: James Braddock corners Max Baer in June 1935. To the surprise of all, Braddock won on points with the odds 10 to 1 against.

Middleweight

	WBC	WBA	IBF	WBO
1978	Hugo Corro (3)	Hugo Corro (3)	—	—
1979	Vito Antuofermo (2)	Vito Antuofermo (2)	—	—
1980	Alan Minter (2)/	Alan Minter (2)/	—	—
	Marvin Hagler (1)	Marvin Hagler (1)		
1981	Marvin Hagler (3)	Marvin Hagler (3)	—	—
1982	Marvin Hagler (2)	Marvin Hagler (2)	—	—
1983	Marvin Hagler (3)	Marvin Hagler (3)	—	—
1984	Marvin Hagler (2)	Marvin Hagler (2)	—	—
1985	Marvin Hagler (1)	Marvin Hagler (1)	—	—
1986	Marvin Hagler (1)	Marvin Hagler (1)	—	—
1987	Sugar Ray Leonard (1)/	Sumbu Kalambay (1)	Sugar Ray Leonard (1)/	—
	Thomas Hearns (1)		Frank Tate (1)	
1988	Iran Barkley (1)	Sumbu Kalambay (3)	Frank Tate (1)/	—
			Michael Nunn (2)	
1989	Roberto Duran (1)	Mike McCallum (1)	Michael Nunn (2)	Doug DeWitt (1)
1990	Julian Jackson (1)	Mike McCallum (2)	Michael Nunn (2)	Doug DeWitt (1)/
				Nigel Benn (2)/
				Chris Eubank (1)
1991	Julian Jackson (1)	Mike McCallum (1)	James Toney (4)	Chris Eubank (3)/
				Gerald McClellan (1)
1992	Julian Jackson (3)	Reggie Johnson (2)	James Toney (3)	Gerald McClellan (0)
1993	Gerald McClellan (2)	Reggie Johnson (2)/	Roy Jones (1)	Chris Pyatt (2)
		John David Jackson (1)		
1994	Gerald McClellan (2)	Jorge Castro (3)	Roy Jones (1)/	Chris Pyatt (1)/
			Bernard Hopkins (1)	Steve Collins (1)
1995	Julian Jackson (1)/	Jorge Castro (2)/	Bernard Hopkins (1)	Lonnie Bradley (2)
	Quincy Taylor (1)	Shinji Takehara (1)		
1996	Keith Holmes (2)	William Joppy (2)	Bernard Hopkins (3)	Lonnie Bradley (? + 1)
1997			Bernard Hopkins (1)	Lonnie Bradley (1)

Light-Middleweight

	WBC	WBA	IBF	WBO
1978	Rocky Mattioli (2)	Masashi Kudo (2)	—	—
1979	Maurice Hope (2)	Masashi Kudo (2)/ Ayub Kalule (2)	—	—
1980	Maurice Hope (2)	Ayub Kalule (3)	—	—
1981	Wilfred Benitez (2)	Sugar Ray Leonard (1)/ Tadashi Mihara (1)	—	—
1982	Wilfred Benitez (1)/ Thomas Hearns (1)	Davey Moore (3)	—	—
1983	Thomas Hearns (0)	Davey Moore (1)/ Roberto Duran (1)	—	—
1984	Thomas Hearns (3)	Mike McCallum (2)	Mark Medal (1)/ Carlos Santos (1)	—
1985	Thomas Hearns (0)	Mike McCallum (1)	Carlos Santos (1)	—
1986	Thomas Hearns (1)/ Duane Thomas (1)	Mike McCallum (2)	Buster Drayton (2)	—
1987	Lupe Aquino (1)/ Gianfranco Rosi (1)	Mike McCallum (2)/ Julian Jackson (1)	Buster Drayton (1)/ Matthew Hilton (2)	—
1988	Gianfranco Rosi (1)/ Don Curry (1)	Julian Jackson (1)	Robert Hines (1)	John David Jackson (1)
1989	Rene Jacquot (1)/ John Mugabi (1)	Julian Jackson (2)	Darrin van Horn (1)/ Gianfranco Rosi (2)	John David Jackson (1)
1990	Terry Norris (2)	Julian Jackson (0)	Gianfranco Rosi (3)	John David Jackson (2)
1991	Terry Norris (4)	Gilbert Dele (2)/ Vinny Pazienza (1)	Gianfranco Rosi (3)	John David Jackson (1)
1992	Terry Norris (2)	Julio Cesar Vasquez (1)	Gianfranco Rosi (2)	John David Jackson (2)
1993	Terry Norris (3)/ Simon Brown (1)	Julio Cesar Vasquez (3)	Gianfranco Rosi (1)	Verno Phillips (1)
1994	Simon Brown (1)/ Terry Norris (1)/ Luis Santana (1)	Julio Cesar Vasquez (6)	Gianfranco Rosi (1)/ Vincent Pettway (1)	Verno Phillips (2)
1995	Luis Santana (1)/ Terry Norris (3)	Pernell Whitaker (1)/ Carl Daniels (1)/ Julio Cesar Vasquez (1)	Vincent Pettway (1)/ Paul Vaden (1)/ Terry Norris (1)	Verno Phillips (1)/ Gianfranco Rosi (1)/ Paul Jones (1)
1996	Terry Norris (2)	Laurent Boudouani (1)	Terry Norris (3)	Ronald Wright (? + 1)
1997	Terry Norris (1)	Laurent Boudouani (1)	Terry Norris (1)/ Raul Marquez (1)	

Welterweight

	WBC	WBA	IBF	WBO
1978	Carlos Palomino (3)	Jose Pipino Cuevas (3)	—	—
1979	Wilfred Benitez (2)/ Sugar Ray Leonard (1)	Jose Pipino Cuevas (3)	—	—
1980	Sugar Ray Leonard (1)/ Roberto Duran (1)/ Sugar Ray Leonard (1)	Jose Pipino Cuevas (1)/ Thomas Hearns (2)	—	—
1981	Sugar Ray Leonard (2)	Thomas Hearns (2)/ Sugar Ray Leonard (1)	—	—
1982	Sugar Ray Leonard (1)	Sugar Ray Leonard (1)	—	—
1983	Milton McCrory (2)	Don Curry (2)	—	—
1984	Milton McCrory (2)	Don Curry (3)	—	—
1985	Milton McCrory (2)/ Don Curry (1)	Don Curry (2)	—	—
1986	Don Curry (1)/ Lloyd Honeyghan (1)	Don Curry (1)/ Lloyd Honeyghan (1)	Lloyd Honeyghan (1)	—
1987	Lloyd Honeyghan (3)/ Jorge Vaca (1)	Mark Breland (1)/ Marlon Starling (1)	Lloyd Honeyghan (3)/ Jorge Vaca (1)	—
1988	Lloyd Honeyghan (2)	Marlon Starling (2)/ Thomas Molinares (1)	Simon Brown (3)	—
1989	Marlon Starling (2)	Mark Breland (4)	Simon Brown (4)	Genaro Leon (1)/ Manning Galloway (1)
1990	Maurice Blocker (1)	Mark Breland (1)/ Aaron Davis (1)	Simon Brown (1)	Manning Galloway (1)
1991	Simon Brown (1)/ James 'Buddy' McGirt (1)	Meldrick Taylor (2)	Maurice Blocker (1)	Manning Galloway (4)
1992	James 'Buddy' McGirt (1)	Meldrick Taylor (1)/ Cristano Espana (1)	Maurice Blocker (1)	Manning Galloway (2)
1993	James 'Buddy' McGirt (1)/ Pernell Whitaker (2)	Cristano Espana (2)	Felix Trinidad (3)	Gert Bo Jacobsen (1)/ Eamonn Loughran (1)
1994	Pernell Whitaker (2)	Ike Quartey (2)	Felix Trinidad (3)	Eamonn Loughran (2)
1995	Pernell Whitaker (2)	Ike Quartey (2)	Felix Trinidad (2)	Eamonn Loughran (3)
1996	Pernell Whitaker (2)	Ike Quartey (2)	Felix Trinidad (3)	Jose Luis Lopez (? + 1)
1997	Pernell Whitaker (1)/ Oscar De La Hoya (1)	Ike Quartey (1)	Felix Trinidad (1)	Michael Loewe (1)

Light-Welterweight

	WBC	WBA	IBF	WBO
1978	Saensak Muangsurin (1)/ Kim Sang Hyun (1)	Antonio Cervantes (2)	—	—
1979	Kim Sang Hyun (2)	Antonio Cervantes (2)	—	—
1980	Saoul Mamby (3)	Antonio Cervantes (1)/ Aaron Pryor (2)	—	—
1981	Saoul Mamby (3)	Aaron Pryor (2)	—	—
1982	Leory Haley (2)	Aaron Pryor (3)	—	—
1983	Leory Haley (1)/ Bruce Curry (3)	Aaron Pryor (2)	—	—
1984	Bill Costello (3)	Johnny Bumphus (1)/ Gene Hatcher (2)	Aaron Pryor (1)	—
1985	Bill Costello (1)/ Lonnie Smith (1)	Ubaldo Sacco (1)	Aaron Pryor (1)	—
1986	Rene Arrendondo (1)/ Tsuyoshi Hamada (2)	Patrizio Oliva (2)	Gary Hinton (1)/ Joe Manley (1)	—
1987	Rene Arrendondo (1)/ Roger Mayweather (1)	Patrizio Oliva (1)/ Juan Martin Coggi (1)	Terry Marsh (2)	—
1988	Roger Mayweather (4)	Juan Martin Coggi (1)	James 'Buddy' McGirt (2)/ Meldrick Taylor (1)	—
1989	Julio Cesar Chavez (3)	Juan Martin Coggi (2)	Meldrick Taylor (3)	Hector Camacho (1)
1990	Julio Cesar Chavez (2)	Juan Martin Coggi (1)/ Loreto Garza (2)	Julio Cesar Chavez (2)	Hector Camacho (2)
1991	Julio Cesar Chavez (2)	Edwin Rosario (1)	Julio Cesar Chavez (1)/ Rafael Pineda (1)	Greg Haugen (1)/ Hector Camacho (1)
1992	Julio Cesar Chavez (3)	Akinobu Hiranaka (1)/ Morris East (1)	Rafael Pineda (1)/ Pernell Whitaker (1)	Carlos Gonzalez (3)
1993	Julio Cesar Chavez (3)	Juan Martin Coggi (6)	Charles Murray (3)	Carlos Gonzalez (1)/ Zack Padilla (3)
1994	Frankie Randall (1)/ Julio Cesar Chavez (3)	Juan Martin Coggi (1)/ Frankie Randall (2)	Jake Rodriguez (3)	Zack Padilla (2)
1995	Julio Cesar Chavez (2)	Frankie Randall (1)	Konstantin Tszyu (2)	Sammy Fuentes (2)
1996	Oscar De La Hoya (1)	Juan Coggi (1)/ Frankie Randall (1)	Konstantin Tszyu (3)	Giovanni Parisi (? +1)
1997	Oscar De La Hoya (1)	Khalid Rahilou (1)	Konstantin Tszyu (1)	Giovanni Parisi (1)

Lightweight

	WBC	WBA	IBF	WBO
1978	Roberto Duran (1)	Roberto Duran (1)	—	—
1979	Jim Watt (2)	Ernesto Espana (2)	—	—
1980	Jim Watt (3)	Hilmer Kenty (4)	—	—
1981	Alexis Arguello (3)	Sean O'Grady (1)/ Claude Noel (1)/ Arturo Frias (1)	—	—
1982	Alexis Arguello (2)	Arturo Frias (1)/ Ray Mancini (3)	—	—
1983	Edwin Rosario (1)	Ray Mancini (1)	—	—
1984	Edwin Rosario (2)/ Jose Luis Ramirez (1)	Ray Mancini (1)/ Livingstone Bramble (1)	Charlie 'Choo Choo' Brown (1)/ Harry Arroyo (2)	—
1985	Hector Camacho (1)	Livingstone Bramble (1)	Harry Arroyo (1)/ Jimmy Paul (2)	—
1986	Hector Camacho (2)	Livingstone Bramble (1)/ Edwin Rosario (1)	Jimmy Paul (2)/ Greg Haugen (1)	—
1987	Jose Luis Ramirez (2)	Edwin Rosario (1)/ Julio Cesar Chavez (1)	Vinny Pazienza (1)	—
1988	Jose Luis Ramirez (1)/ Julio Cesar Chavez (1)	Julio Cesar Chavez (2)	Greg Haugen (3)	—
1989	Pernell Whitaker (1)	Edwin Rosario (1)	Pernell Whitaker (3)	Mauricio Aceves (3)
1990	Pernell Whitaker (3)	Juan Nazario (1)/ Pernell Whitaker (1)	Pernell Whitaker (3)	Dingaan Thobela (1)
1991	Pernell Whitaker (3)	Pernell Whitaker (3)	Pernell Whitaker (3)	Dingaan Thobela (2)
1992	Miguel Angel Gonzalez (2)	Joey Gamache (1)/ Tony Lopez (1)	Fred Pendleton (1)	Giovanni Parisi (1)
1993	Miguel Angel Gonzalez (3)	Tony Lopez (1)/ Dingaan Thobela (1)/ Orzoubek Nazarov (1)	Fred Pendleton (2)	Giovanni Parisi (2)
1994	Miguel Angel Gonzalez (3)	Orzoubek Nazarov (2)	Rafael Ruelas (2)	Oscar De La Hoya (3)
1995	Miguel Angel Gonzalez (3)	Orzoubek Nazarov (2)	Rafael Ruelas (1)/ Oscar De La Hoya (1)/ Phillip Holiday (2)	Oscar De La Hoya (4)
1996	Jean-Baptiste Mendy (1)	Orzoubek Nazarov (12)	Phillip Holiday (4)	Artur Gregorian (? + 2)
1997	Stevie Johnston (1)			Artur Gregorian (1)

Super-Featherweight

	WBC	WBA	IBF	WBO
1978	Alexis Arguello (4)	Sam Serrano (3)	—	—
1979	Alexis Arguello (3)	Sam Serrano (2)	—	—
1980	Alexis Arguello (2)/ Rafael Limon (1)	Sam Serrano (1)/ Yasutsune Uehara (2)	—	—
1981	Cornelius Boza-Edwards (2)/ Rolando Navarette (1)	Sam Serrano (3)	—	—
1982	Rolando Navarette (1)/ Rafael Limon (2)/ Bobby Chacon (1)	Sam Serrano (1)	—	—
1983	Bobby Chacon (1)/ Hector Camacho (1)	Roger Mayweather (3)	—	—
1984	Julio Cesar Chavez (1)	Rocky Lockridge (2)	Hwan-Kil Yuh (2)	—
1985	Julio Cesar Chavez (3)	Rocky Lockridge (1)/ Wilfredo Gomez (1)	Lester Ellis (2)/ Barry Michael (2)	—
1986	Julio Cesar Chavez (4)	Alfredo Layne (1)/ Brian Mitchell (1)	Barry Michael (2)	—
1987	Julio Cesar Chavez (2)	Brian Mitchell (4)	Rocky Lockridge (2)	—
1988	Azumah Nelson (3)	Brian Mitchell (2)	Rocky Lockridge (1)/ Tony Lopez (2)	—
1989	Azumah Nelson (2)	Brian Mitchell (3)	Tony Lopez (2)/ Juan 'John-John' Molina (1)	Juan 'John-John' Molina (1)/ Kamel Bou-Ali (1)
1990	Azumah Nelson (1)	Brian Mitchell (2)	Juan 'John-John' Molina (1)/ Tony Lopez (2)	Kamel Bou-Ali (1)
1991	Azumah Nelson (1)	Brian Mitchell (1)/ Joey Gamache (1)/ Genaro Hernandez (1)	Tony Lopez (1)/ Brian Mitchell	Kamel Bou-Ali (1)
1992	Azumah Nelson (2)	Genaro Hernandez (2)	Juan 'John-John' Molina (2)	Daniel Londas (1)/ Jimmy Bredahl (1)
1993	Azumah Nelson (2)	Genaro Hernandez (3)	Juan 'John-John' Molina (3)	Jimmy Bredahl (1)
1994	Jesse James Leija (1)/ Gabriel Ruelas (1)	Genaro Hernandez (2)	Juan 'John-John' Molina (3)	Oscar De La Hoya (2)/ Regilio Tuur (1)
1995	Gabriel Ruelas (2)/ Azumah Nelson (1)	Yong Soo Choi (1)	Eddie Hopson (1)/ Tracy Harris Patterson (1)/ Arturo Gatti (1)	Regilio Tuur (4)
1996	Azumah Nelson (1)	Yong Soo Choi (3)	Arturo Gatti (1)	Regilio Tuur (? + 1)
1997	Genaro Hernandez (1)		Arturo Gatti (1)	Arnulfo Castillo (1)

RIVIERA

Featherweight

	WBC	WBA	IBF	WBO
1978	Danny Lopez (4)	Eusebio Pedroza (3)	—	—
1979	Danny Lopez (3)	Eusebio Pedroza (4)	—	—
1980	Salvador Sanchez (5)	Eusebio Pedroza (4)	—	—
1981	Salvador Sanchez (3)	Eusebio Pedroza (3)	—	—
1982	Salvador Sanchez (2)/ Juan LaPorte (1)	Eusebio Pedroza (2)	—	—
1983	Juan LaPorte (2)	Eusebio Pedroza (2)	—	—
1984	Wilfredo Gomez (1)/ Azumah Nelson (1)	Eusebio Pedroza (1)	Min-Keun Oh (2)	—
1985	Azumah Nelson (2)	Eusebio Pedroza (1)/ Barry McGuigan (2)	Min-Keun Oh (1)/ Ki-Yung Chung (1)	—
1986	Azumah Nelson (2)	Barry McGuigan (1)/ Steve Cruz (1)	Ki-Yung Chung (2)/ Antonio Rivera (1)	—
1987	Azumah Nelson (2)	Antonio Esparragoza (2)	Antonio Rivera (0)	—
1988	Jeff Fenech (3)	Antonio Esparragoza (2)	Calvin Grove (2)/ Jorge Paez (1)	—
1989	Jeff Fenech (1)	Antonio Esparragoza (3)	Jorge Paez (5)	Maurizio Stecca (2)/ Louie Espinosa (1)
1990	Marcos Villasana (2)	Antonio Esparragoza (1)	Jorge Paez (3)	Jorge Paez (2)
1991	Marcos Villasana (2)/ Paul Hodkinson (1)	Kyun-Yung Park (3)	Troy Dorsey (1)/ Manuel Medina (2)	Maurizio Stecca (3)
1992	Paul Hodkinson (2)	Kyun-Yung Park (4)	Manuel Medina (3)	Colin McMillan (1)/ Ruben Palacio (1)
1993	Paul Hodkinson (1)/ Gregorio Vargas (1)/ Kevin Kelley (1)	Kyun-Yung Park (2)/ Eloy Rojas (1)	Tom Johnson (3)	Steve Robinson (3)
1994	Kevin Kelley (1)	Eloy Rojas (3)	Tom Johnson (3)	Steve Robinson (3)
1995	Alejandro Gonzalez (3)/ Manuel Medina (1)/ Luisito Espinosa (1)	Eloy Rojas (2)	Tom Johnson (3)	Steve Robinson (2)/ Prince Naseem Hamed (1)
1996	Luisito Espinosa (3)	Eloy Rojas (1)/ Wilfredo Vazquez (2)	Tom Johnson (3)	Prince Naseem Hamed (4)
1997			Prince Naseem Hamed (1)	Prince Naseem Hamed (1)

Super-Bantamweight

	WBC	WBA	IBF	WBO
1978	Wilfredo Gomez (5)	Soo Hwan Hong (1)/	—	—
		Ricardo Cardona (3)		
1979	Wilfredo Gomez (4)	Ricardo Cardona (3)	—	—
1980	Wilfredo Gomez (3)	Leo Randolph (1)/	—	—
		Sergio Palma (2)		
1981	Wilfredo Gomez (0)	Sergio Palma (3)	—	—
1982	Wilfredo Gomez (4)	Sergio Palma (1)/	—	—
		Leonard Cruz (2)		
1983	Jaime Garza (1)	Leonard Cruz (2)	Bobby Berna (1)	—
1984	Jaime Garza (1)/	Loris Stecca (1)/	Seung-In Suh (2)	—
	Juan Meza (1)	Victor Callejas (1)		
1985	Juan Meza (1)/	Victor Callejas (2)	Ji-Won Kim (4)	—
	Lupe Pintor (1)			
1986	Samart Payakarun (2)	Victor Callejas (0)	Ji-Won Kim (1)	—
1987	Jeff Fenech (3)	Louie Espinosa (3)/	Seung-Hoon Lee (4)	—
		Julio Gervacio (1)		
1988	Daniel Zaragoza (3)	Bernardo Pinango (1)/	Jose Sanabria (4)	—
		Juan Jose Estrada (2)		
1989	Daniel Zaragoza (3)	Juan Jose Estrada (2)/	Fabrice Benichou (3)	Kenny Mitchell (2)/
		Jesus Salud (1)		Valerio Nati (1)
1990	Paul Banke (2)/	Luis Mendoza (3)	Welcome Ncita (3)	Orlando Fernandez (1)
	Pedro Decima (1)			
1991	Kiyoshi Hatanaka (1)/	Luis Mendoza (3)/	Welcome Ncita (3)	Jesse Benavides (2)
	Daniel Zaragoza (3)	Raul Perez (1)		
1992	Thierry Jacob (1)/	Wilfredo Vasquez (3)	Welcome Ncita (1)/	Duke McKenzie (1)
	Tracy Harris Patterson (2)		Kennedy McKinney (1)	
1993	Tracy Harris Patterson (1)	Wilfredo Vasquez (3)	Kennedy McKinney (2)	Daniel Jiminez (2)
1994	Tracy Harris Patterson (1)/	Wilfredo Vasquez (3)	Kennedy McKinney (1)/	Daniel Jiminez (3)
	Hector Acero Sanchez (1)		Vuyani Bungu (2)	
1995	Hector Acero Sanchez (2)/	Wilfredo Vasquez (1)/	Vuyani Bungu (3)	Marco Antonio Barrera (5)
	Daniel Zaragoza (1)	Antonio Cermeno (2)		
1996	Daniel Zaragoza (2)	Antonio Cermeno (3)	Vuyani Bungu (3)	Marco Antonio Barrera (? + 2)/
				Junior Jones (1)
1997	Daniel Zaragoza (1)	Daniel Zaragoza (1)	Vuyani Bungu (1)	Junior Jones (1)

Bantamweight

	WBC	WBA	IBF	WBO
1978	Carlos Zarate (3)	Jorge Lujan (2)	—	—
1979	Carlos Zarate (1)/ Lupe Pintor (1)	Jorge Lujan (2)	—	—
1980	Lupe Pintor (4)	Jorge Lujan (1)/ Julian Solis (1)/ Jeff Chandler (1)	—	—
1981	Lupe Pintor (3)	Jeff Chandler (4)	—	—
1982	Lupe Pintor (1)	Jeff Chandler (2)	—	—
1983	Albert Davila (1)	Jeff Chandler (3)	—	—
1984	Albert Davila (1)	Richard Sandoval (3)	Satoshi Shingaki (2)	—
1985	Daniel Zaragoza (1)/ Miguel Lora (1)	Richard Sandoval (0)	Jeff Fenech (3)	—
1986	Miguel Lora (3)	Gaby Canizales (1)/ Bernardo Pinango (3)	Jeff Fenech (1)	—
1987	Miguel Lora (2)	Bernardo Pinango (1)/ Takuya Muguruma (1)/ Chan-Yong Park (1)/ Wilfredo Vasquez (1)	Kelvin Seabrooks (3)	—
1988	Miguel Lora (2)/ Raul Perez (1)	Wilfredo Vasquez (1)/ Kaokor Galaxy (1)/ Sung-Il Moon (2)	Kelvin Seabrooks (1)/ Orlando Canizales (2)	—
1989	Raul Perez (3)	Sung-Il Moon (1)/ Kaokor Galaxy (1)/ Luisito Espinosa (1)	Orlando Canizales (1)	Israel Conterras (1)
1990	Raul Perez (3)	Luisito Espinosa (3)	Orlando Canizales (3)	Israel Conterras (1)
1991	Greg Richardson (2)/ Joichiro Tatsuyushi (1)	Israel Conterras (1)	Orlando Canizales (3)	Gaby Canizales (1)/ Duke McKenzie (2)
1992	Victor Rabanales (4)	Eddie Cook (1)/ Jorge Elicier Julio (2)	Orlando Canizales (2)	Duke McKenzie (1)/ Rafael Del Valle (1)
1993	Victor Rabanales (1)/ Jung-Il Byun (2)/ Yasuei Yakushiji (1)	Junior Jones (1)	Orlando Canizales (3)	Rafael Del Valle (2)
1994	Yasuei Yakushiji (3)	Junior Jones (1)/ John Michael Johnson (1)/ Daorung Chuvatana (2)	Orlando Canizales (3)	Alfred Kotey (2)
1995	Yasuei Yakushiji (1)/ Wayne McCullough (2)	Daorung Chuvatana (1)/ Veeraphol Sahaprom (1)	Harold Mestre (1)/ Mbulelo Botile (3)	Alfred Kotey (1)/ Daniel Jiminez (1)
1996	Wayne McCullough (1)	Nana Konadu (1)/ Sirimongkol Singmanasuk (1)/ Daorung Chuvatana (1)	Mbulelo Botile (3)	
1997	Sirimongkol Singmanasuk (2)	Daorung Chuvatana (1)		

Super-Flyweight

	WBC	WBA	IBF	WBO
1980	Rafael Orono (4)	—	—	—
1981	Chul-Ho Kim (4)	Gustavo Ballas (1)/ Rafael Pedroza (1)	—	—
1982	Chul-Ho Kim (2)/ Rafael Orono (1)	Jiro Watanabe (3)	—	—
1983	Rafael Orono (3)/ Payao Poontarat (1)	Jiro Watanabe (3)	Joo-Do Chun (1)	—
1984	Payao Poontarat (1)/ Jiro Watanabe (2)	Jiro Watanabe (2)/ Kaosai Galaxy (1)	Joo-Do Chun (4)	—
1985	Jiro Watanabe (3)	Kaosai Galaxy (3)	Joo-Do Chun (1)/ Elly Pical (2)	—
1986	Gilberto Roman (5)	Kaosai Galaxy (1)	Carlos Cesar Polanco (1)/ Elly Pical (2)	—
1987	Gilberto Roman (2)/ Santos Laciar (1)/ Sugar Baby Rojas (2)	Kaosai Galaxy (2)	Tae-Il Chang (1)/ Elly Pical (1)	—
1988	Gilberto Roman (4)	Kaosai Galaxy (2)	Elly Pical (2)	—
1989	Gilberto Roman (2)/ Nana Yaw Konadu (1)	Kaosai Galaxy (4)	Elly Pical (1)/ Juan Polo Perez (1)	Jose Ruiz (2)
1990	Sung-Il Moon (3)	Kaosai Galaxy (3)	Robert Quiroga (2)	Jose Ruiz (2)
1991	Sung-Il Moon (3)	Kaosai Galaxy (3)	Robert Quiroga (2)	Jose Ruiz (0)
1992	Sung-Il Moon (2)	Katsuya Onizuka (2)	Robert Quiroga (2)	Jose Quirino (1)/ Johnny Bredahl (1)
1993	Sung-Il Moon (2)/ Jose Luis Bueno (1)	Katsuya Onizuka (2)	Julio Cesar Borboa (4)	Johnny Bredahl (2)
1994	Hiroshi Kawashima (2)	Katsuya Onizuka (1)/ Hyung-Chul Lee (1)	Julio Cesar Borboa (2)/ Harold Grey (2)	Johnny Bredahl (1)/ Johnny Tapia (1)
1995	Hiroshi Kawashima (3)	Hyung-Chul Lee (1)/ Alimi Goitia (2)	Harold Grey (2)/ Carlos Salazar (1)	Johnny Tapia (4)
1996	Hiroshi Kawashima (2)	Alimi Goitia (2)/	Carlos Salazar (1)/	Johnny Tapia (? + 4)
1997	Gerry Penalosa (1)		Danny Romero (1)	Johnny Tapia (1)

Flyweight

	WBC	WBA	IBF	WBO
1978	Miguel Canto (3)	Guty Espadas (1)/ Betulio Gonzalez (2)	—	—
1979	Miguel Canto (1)/ Chan Hee Park (4)	Betulio Gonzalez (2)/ Luis Ibarra (1)	—	—
1980	Chan Hee Park (2)/ Shoji Oguma (3)	Taeshik Kim (2)/ Peter Mathebula (1)	—	—
1981	Shoji Oguma (1)/ Antonio Avelar (2)	Santos Laciar (1)/ Luis Ibarra (1)/ Juan Herrera (2)	—	—
1982	Prudencio Cardona (1)/ Freddie Castillo (1)/ Eleoncio Mercedes (1)	Santos Laciar (3)	—	—
1983	Charlie Magri (1)/ Frank Cedeno (1)	Santos Laciar (3)	Soon-Chun Kwon (1)	—
1984	Koji Kobayashi (1)/ Gabriel Bernal (2)/ Sot Chitalada (1)	Santos Laciar (3)	Soon-Chun Kwon (3)	—
1985	Sot Chitalada (2)	Santos Laciar (1)/ Hilario Zapata (1)	Soon-Chun Kwon (3)/ Chong-Kwang Chung (1)	—
1986	Sot Chitalada (2)	Hilario Zapata (5)	Bi-Won Chung (1)/ Hi-Sup Shin (2)	—
1987	Sot Chitalada (1)	Fidel Bassa (4)	Dodie Penalosa (1)/ Chang-Ho Choi (1)	—
1988	Sot Chitalada (1)/ Yong-Kang Kim (2)	Fidel Bassa (2)	Rolando Bohol (2)/ Duke McKenzie (1)	—
1989	Yong-Kang Kim (1)/ Sot Chitalada (1)	Fidel Bassa (1)/ Jesus Rojas (1)	Duke McKenzie (1)/ Dave McAuley (2)	Elvis Alvarez (1)
1990	Sot Chitalada (4)	Yul-Woo Lee (1)/ Yukihito Tamakuma (2)	Dave McAuley (2)	Isidro Perez (2)
1991	Muangchai Kitikasem (3)	Elvis Alvarez (1)/ Yong-Kang Kim (2)	Dave McAuley (2)	Isidro Perez (1)
1992	Muangchai Kitikasem (1)/ Yuri Arbachakov (2)	Yong-Kang Kim (1)/ Aquiles Guzman (1)/ David Griman (1)	Rodolfo Blanco (1)/ Pichit Sitbangprachan (1)	Pat Clinton (2)
1993	Yuri Arbachakov (3)	David Griman (2)	Pichit Sitbangprachan (2)	Jake Matlala (2)
1994	Yuri Arbachakov (1)	Saensor Ploenchit (5)	Pichit Sitbangprachan (2)	Jake Matlala (2)
1995	Yuri Arbachakov (2)	Saensor Ploenchit (2)	Francisco Tejedor (1)/ Danny Romero (2)	Alberto Jiminez (3)
1996	Yuri Arbachakov (2)	Saensor Ploenchit (3)/ Jose Bonilla (1)	Mark Johnson (2)	Alberto Jiminez (? + 2)/ Carlos Salazar (1)
1997		Jose Bonilla (1)	Mark Johnson (1)	Carlos Salazar (1)

Light-Flyweight

	WBC	WBA	IBF	WBO
1978	Freddie Castillo (1)/ Netrnoi Vorasingh (2)/ Sung-Jun Kim (1)	Yoko Gushiken (3)	—	—
1979	Sung-Jun Kim (3)	Yoko Gushiken (4)	—	—
1980	Shigeo Nakajima (1)/ Hilario Zapata (5)	Yoko Gushiken (3)	—	—
1981	Hilario Zapata (4)	Pedro Flores (1)/ Hwan-Jin Kim (2)/ Katsuo Tokashiki (1)	—	—
1982	Amado Ursua (1)/ Tadashi Tomori (1)/ Hilario Zapata (2)	Katsuo Tokashiki (3)	—	—
1983	Jung Koo Chang (3)	Katsuo Tokashiki (2)/ Lupe Madera (2)	Dodie Penalosa (1)	—
1984	Jung Koo Chang (3)	Francisco Quiroz (2)	Dodie Penalosa (2)	—
1985	Jung Koo Chang 2)	Myung-Woo Yuh (1)	Dodie Penalosa (1)	—
1986	Jung Koo Chang (3)	Myung-Woo Yuh (3)	Jum-Hwan Choi (1)	—
1987	Jung Koo Chang (3)	Myung-Woo Yuh (3)	Jum-Hwan Choi (3)	—
1988	Jung Koo Chang (1)/ German Torres (1)	Myung-Woo Yuh (4)	Tacy Macalos (1)	—
1989	Yul-Woo Lee (1)/ Humberto Gonzalez (2)	Myung-Woo Yuh (3)	Muangchai Kitkasem (2)	Jose De Jesus (2)
1990	Humberto Gonzalez (4)	Myung-Woo Yuh (3)	Muangchai Kitkasem (2)/ Michael Carbajal (2)	Jose De Jesus (2)
1991	Humberto Gonzalez (1)	Myung-Woo Yuh (1)/ Hiroki Ioka (1)	Michael Carbajal (3)	Jose De Jesus (0)
1992	Humberto Gonzalez (4)	Hiroki Ioka (2)/ Myung-Woo Yuh (1)	Michael Carbajal (2)	Josue Camacho (1)
1993	Michael Carbajal (3)	Myung-Woo Yuh (1)/ Leo Gamez (1)	Michael Carbajal (3)	Josue Camacho (0)
1994	Humberto Gonzalez (3)	Leo Gamez (3)	Humberto Gonzalez (3)	Josue Camacho (1)/ Michael Carbajal (1)/ Paul Weir (1)
1995	Humberto Gonzalez (1)/ Saman Sorjaturong (2)	Hiyong Choi (2)	Humberto Gonzalez (1)/ Saman Sorjaturong (2)	Paul Weir (1)/ Jake Matlala (1)
1996	Saman Sorjaturong (5)	Carlos Murillo (2)/ Keiji Yamaguchi (3)	Michael Carbajal (3)	
1997	Saman Sorjaturong (1)		Mauricio Pastrana (1)	Jake Matlala (1)

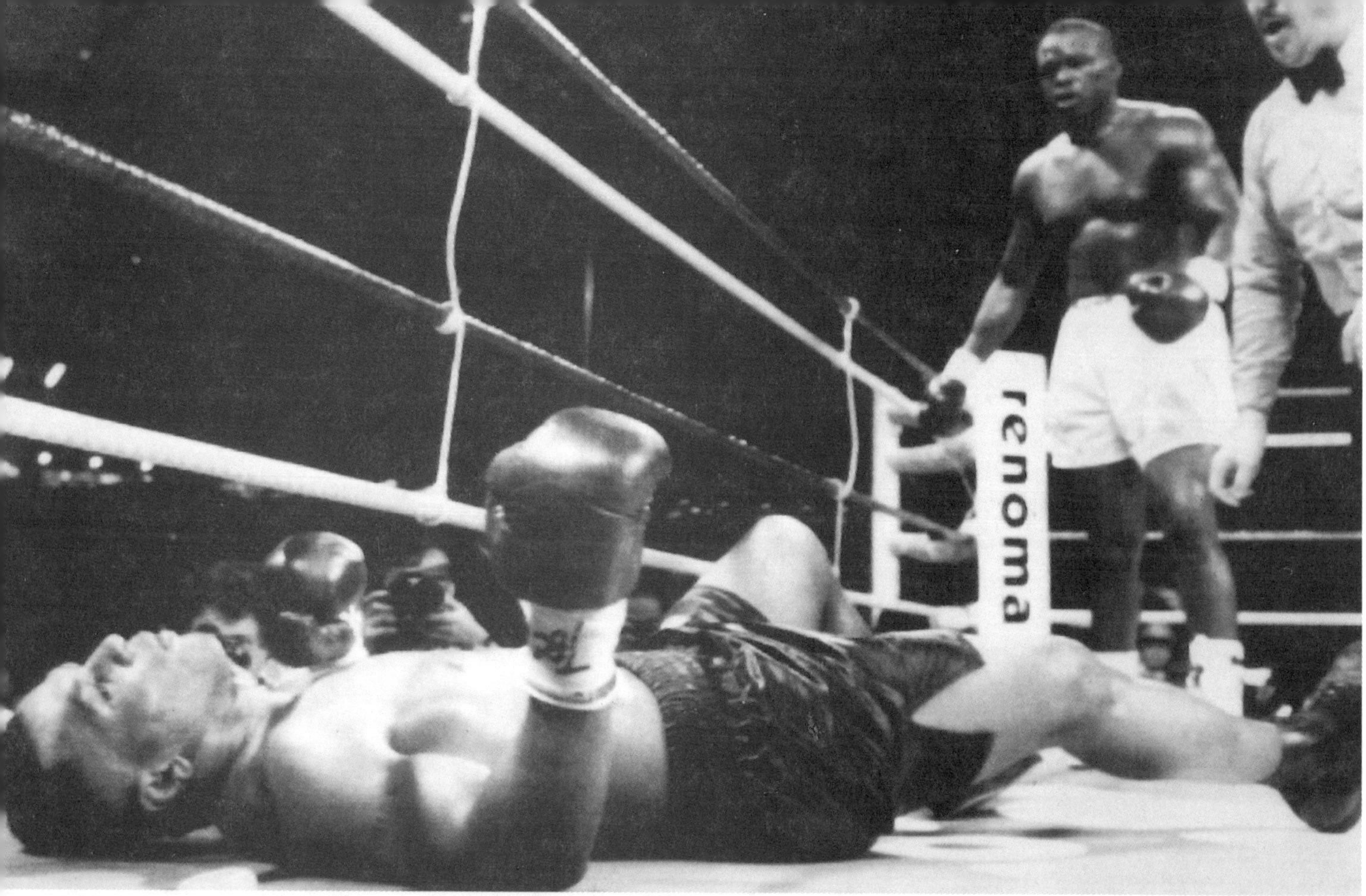

ABOVE: James 'Buster' Douglas's great moment: 'Iron' Mike Tyson lies on the canvas in Tokyo. Shortly afterwards Tyson would be in jail on rape charges. After his release he regained the WBC title from Britain's Frank Bruno and the WBA version from the equally-petrified Bruce Seldon.

RIGHT: Tyson in happier days: it's 1988 and he's the undisputed heavyweight champion of the world.

LEFT: Moorer sprang to fame as a fast and savage puncher, going on to win the WBO light-heavyweight title in 1988 and successfully defending it a record 10 times in four years. He then set off on the road to win the coveted world heavyweight title, fighting for the WBA/IBF title against Evander Holyfield in Las Vegas on 23 April 1993. He won but lost the title the next year to George Foreman.

WBC

Strawweight

	WBC	WBA	IBF	WBO
1987	Hiroki Ioka (1)	—	Kyung-Yun Lee (1)	—
1988	Hiroki Ioka (2)/ Napa Kiatwanchai (1)	Luis Gamez (2)	Samuth Sithnaruepol (2)	—
1989	Napa Kiatwanchai (2)/ Jum-Hwan Choi (1)	Bong-Jun Kim (3)	Samuth Sithnaruepol (1)/ Nico Thomas (1)/ Eric Chavez (1)	Rafael Torres (1)
1990	Hideyuki Ohashi (2)/ Ricardo Lopez (1)	Bong-Jun Kim (3)	Fahlan Lukmingkwan (4)	Rafael Torres (1)
1991	Ricardo Lopez (2)	Hi-Yon Choi (3)	Fahlan Lukmingkwan (2)	Rafael Torres (0)
1992	Ricardo Lopez (3)	Hi-Yon Choi (2)/ Hideyuki Ohashi (1)	Fahlan Lukmingkwan (2)/ Manny Melchor (1)/ Ratanapol Sowvoraphin (1)	Rafael Torres (0)
1993	Ricardo Lopez (3)	Chana Porpaoin (4)	Ratanapol Sowvoraphin (4)	Paul Weir (2)/ Alex Sanchez (1)
1994	Ricardo Lopez (4)	Chana Porpaoin (3)	Ratanapol Sowvoraphin (4)	Alex Sanchez (3)
1995	Ricardo Lopez (1)	Chana Porpaoin (2)/ Rosendo Alvarez (1)	Ratanapol Sowvoraphin (4)	Alex Sanchez (2)
1996	Ricardo Lopez (4)	Rosendo Alvarez (2)	Ratanapol Sowvoraphin (4)	
1997	Ricardo Lopez (1)	Rosendo Alvarez (1)/ Yokthai Sit Oar (1)	Ratanapol Sowvoraphin (1)	Wellington Vicente (1)/ Alex Sanchez (1)